20th Century Silver

Curated by Helen Clifford

Sponsored by LIBERTY

Contents

1 **Foreword** 4

2 **Introduction** 5
Helen Clifford, Curator

3 **Continuity and Change** 6
The craft of the silversmith today
Helen Clifford

4 **Craft and Industry** 24
Eric Turner

5 **Inheriting Modernism** 34
Michael Rowe

6 **Biographies** 37
Silversmiths working today

7 **Exhibition list** 71

8 **Select bibliography** 78

Jug, 1938
Sigvard Bernadotte (Cat. no. 33)
Photo: courtesy of Bröhan-Museum

1 Foreword

Linda Theophilus
Head of Exhibitions

20th Century Silver marks the beginning of a major Crafts Council initiative to develop contemporary silver in this country and to promote the work of today's silversmiths.

Our aims for the exhibition were to provide an historical context for modern silver for the table, and to further inspire both makers and collectors.

To carry out this complex task, we invited Dr Helen Clifford, specialist in the history of silver and an experienced exhibition curator to shape the show. We are most grateful to her for her enthusiastic and energetic response. Her wide ranging research has resulted in an exhibition of work from seventeen countries, the earliest piece dating from 1670. The work of thirty living makers bears witness to their fine design skills and craftsmanship.

We are also most fortunate to have drawn on the experience and knowledge of two specialist advisers, Eric Turner, Assistant Curator, Metalwork Collection, Victoria and Albert Museum, and Michael Rowe, leading maker and Course Leader, Goldsmithing, Silversmithing, Metalwork and Jewellery at the Royal College of Art, both of whom acted as selectors for the contemporary work.

2 **Introduction**
Helen Clifford
Curator

The craft of the silversmith has an ancient and distinguished pedigree. It is perhaps this very reputation which has distanced the craft from today's public. **20th Century Silver** is intended to bring you closer to some of the most inspiring and influential pieces. It is for you to judge how the craft has mirrored stylistic changes, not only in England but in Europe, and what the work of current silversmiths tells us about the culture we live in now.

The Crafts Council has made possible the display of a unique collection of objects. I would like to thank Linda Theophilus, Head of Exhibitions at the Crafts Council for giving me the opportunity of both curating and learning.

The exhibition owes much to the hard work and enthusiasm of Exhibitions Assistant, Hilary Williams. Eric Turner from the Metalwork Collection at the Victoria and Albert Museum has been generous with his time and expertise. Michael Rowe from the Royal College of Art proved a greatly valued advisor. Of all the institutions and individuals who have been so supportive, I would particularly like to thank Rosemary Ransome-Wallis from the Goldsmiths' Company and Annelies Krekel-Aalberse.

3 Continuity & Change
The craft of the silversmith today

Helen Clifford,
formerly Director of the M.A.
in Gallery Studies, Department
of Art History & Theory,
University of Essex, now
Leverhulme Research Fellow at
the Ashmolean Museum, Oxford.

Tête-à-tête, 1930
Maurice Muller (Cat. no. 37)
Photo: courtesy Bröhan-Museum

Silver is a light, malleable and therefore amazingly flexible metal. It is capable of being worked into a variety of forms and decorated with many different techniques. When polished it takes on a brilliantly reflective surface, mirroring its surroundings, which combined with its intrinsic value makes it one of the most desirable materials known to man. The cost of the metal is responsible for the high social status of the material, but also the cause of its downfall, in terms of the survival of historical examples of craftsmanship and its use today. Silverware is an easily portable and convertible source of cash, either literally by melting it down, or through sale, hence its attractiveness as an investment. There is a perpetual interplay between the value of the raw material and the craftsmanship involved in its making.

The stylistic development and social role of silver balances between the forces of continuity and change. Continuity of skills, tools and techniques versus changes in social custom and style, and hence usage. Although the possession and display of silverware is still a symbol of status, it has to vie with a far wider array of material goods than in the past. Historically the table has been a focal point for the definition and exercise of power. Its importance as an indicator of wealth and authority lay not only in the quantity and quality of silver plate but also in its strategic arrangement and use. Today the table is no longer such an important and recognised arena of display.

In more fundamental terms there is a continuity of archetypal forms, which have changed little over the centuries, the prototypes for bowls, plates, cups which George Kubler calls 'prime objects'. Domestic artefacts made in silver are known to survive in quantity from the second millenium BC. These are dishes and drinking vessels manufactured by Mycenean craftsmen, the form of which is still familiar. The individual creation of the object is influenced by a collective intelligence that bypasses the necessity for invention. The ancient solutions to the problems of function interact with the ebb and flow of decorative styles that locate an object in a particular period and place. Changing fashions link the form and ornament of an object to current social, cultural, technical and economic developments.

The basic shapes of hollow ware are familiar to the public through intimate use and a history of form which is recognisable over centuries. We come to them with expectations, formed by past experiences of these objects. The craftsman can confirm this pre-knowledge, with a conservative design, or these expectations can be challenged, manipulating our vision of the familiar. 'The starting point for creating a form' explains the Danish silversmith Allan Scharff 'is the use of existing form combinations, setting them together and altering them. Or putting it another way, combining a series of familiar form sections into a new form, just as a mathematician works with numbers or a physicist with raw materials'. The translation of the 'necessary' utensil into a luxury product is at the centre of a very complex set of inter-relationships.

If a medieval silversmith were to be suddenly transported forward through time into the workshop of a modern maker he would find himself very much at home. The twelfth century working manual *De Diversis Artibus*, describes metalworking techniques still commonly used today. The basic processes of forming silver, blocking, raising, casting, box-making and hand-forging have changed little over the centuries. With the exception of electro-forming, die-stamping and spinning, the techniques used by the modern silversmith go back at least as far as the first clearly defined development of the craft in the middle of the third millennium BC. Modern technology has provided powered mechanical aids to enable some of these techniques to be carried out with less physical effort and less dependence on personal skill.

The mass production of goods, and particularly of cheaply stamped silverware in the nineteenth century has over-emphasised the changes, rather than the continuity in the craft. What has resulted is a polarization in the popular imagination between hand-makers and mass-manufacturers. Henry Wilson in his *Textbook for Students and Workers in Metal* (1902) wrote of the 'touching witness to the spirit of the worker' which was evident in the work of a single craftsman, who oversaw the whole production process, from design and construction to decoration. An image of the working silversmith as an independent craftsman, the descendant of the medieval guild master was thus elaborated, if not invented and is our powerful inheritance from the Arts and Crafts Movement. In fact it was rare for a piece of silver to be made entirely by the same hand, for although the fully trained silversmith was often proficient in all branches of the trade, it was common practice to use specialists in such skills as engraving, casting or die-cutting, whether retained by the smith, or employed on a 'free-lance' basis. Mechanised production

implied the severance of the individual from the whole process of manufacture, and an increasing separation of the working silversmith from the customer who was ultimately buying the goods.

Other commentators saw no reason why silver-ware could not still be beautiful and be made by machine. Many of Christopher Dresser's highly original shapes arose out of a dual concern with the techniques of machine production and with the function of the articles he designed. Design took precedence over craftsmanship. As with William Morris, although coming from a different direction, he linked methods of production to a social conscience. Because silver was synonymous with the expensive and precious, Dresser designed forms which could be produced in both silver and much cheaper electro-plate.

Dresser believed that 'Silver objects, like those formed of clay or glass, should perfectly serve the end for which they have been formed… Silver and gold being materials of considerable worth, it is necessary that the utmost economy be observed in using them. If the designer forms works which are expensive, he places them beyond the reach of those who might otherwise enjoy them'.

Although Modernists, of whom Dresser was an inspired forerunner, believed that a break with the past would hasten a renewal of art, as well as contributing to progress and innovation in society, it is clear that their aims owed much to earlier ideas. Functionalism, a belief that form was derived from use, which was integral to the International Modern Style has a very ancient history. The 1930s Modernists quoted from Plato, 'By beauty of shapes… I mean straight lines and circles, and shapes, plane or solid, made from them by lathe, rule or square. These are not like other things, beautiful relatively, but always and absolutely'. Modernist designers tended to employ a minimum of parts in the handling of form, often fusing elements to create a single strong profile. If one compares the Berkeley tea pot of 1670 with Chris Knight's water pitchers made in 1992, both using simple and functional cone construction it is clear how universal and everlasting these forms are. As Chris Knight has commented 'for the silversmith these functional requirements should not be regarded as restrictions upon creativity, but merely creative guidelines'.

Modern times demanded modern means, and the machine seemed the most appropriate representative of modernity. The Bauhaus, which assigned priority to

Below: *Wine ewer, 1933*
Svend Weihrauch (Cat. no. 32)
Photo: courtesy Bröhan-Museum

Opposite: *Jug, 1925*
Johan Rohde (Cat. no. 27)

*The Berkeley Teapot, 1670/71
(Cat. no. 1) Photo: courtesy of the
Victoria and Albert Museum*

machine production in the search for a universal language of forms that would remove all social and national barriers, marked the culmination of this pro-machine ideology. Marianne Brandt's tea infuser is a transitional piece. It reveals, in its hand-hammered construction an older allegiance to an Arts and Crafts tradition (fostered by Christian Dell), combined with a new concern for producing industrial models (the priority for Lazlo Moholy-Nagy). Ironically, in the words of Willhelm Wagenfeld, who took over as director of the Bauhaus metal workshop from Brandt, 'the metalwork designs at the Bauhaus, which looked as though they could be made inexpensively by machine techniques were, in fact, extremely costly craft designs'.

The complicated relationship between craft and mechanised techniques in the realisation of function-alism can also be seen in the work of the Parisian silversmith Jean Puiforçat. He believed that

'What we need today are utilitarian objects without ornamentation, that are not disguised as something else, although this does not prevent their being refined as pieces of great value. The form imposed by its ultimate function is the object's permanent element. The desire to create a form of expression out of that form is what gives the object its constantly changing character.'

Like the designers of the Bauhaus, Puiforçat based his new forms on the sphere, the cone and the cylinder, but the results are very different. Despite remarking that 'Silverwork has beautifully polished metal in common with the machine', these objects with large undecorated surfaces and sharp angles could only be made by skilled craftsmen. They were objects de luxe.

When we turn from production to consumption the forces of change are perhaps more dramatically evident. In 1798 the German visitor to England, Sophie von la Roche delighted in the novelty of being able to compare 'the silver work of previous genera-tions with up-to-date modern creations' in Thomas Jefferies' shop. Here 'the clients' taste and artists' workmanship at different periods may be construed and criticised'. During the nineteenth century the status of 'old' silver rose, stimulated by the exhibitions of antiques held from 1840s. As a result institutions and individuals commissioning plate turned increasingly to copies of antiques. Charles Eastlake in his *Hints on Household Taste*, (1867) recommended visiting 'the old jewellery-shops in Hanway Street and Wardour

Tea-infuser (with strainer), 1924
Marianne Brandt (Cat. no. 22)
Photo: courtesy of the British Museum

16

Orange juice dispenser, 1930
Jean Puiforçat (Cat. no. 35)
Photo: courtesy of Bröhan Museum

Tureen, 1937
Jean Puiforçat (Cat. no. 36)
Photo: courtesy of Bröhan-Museum

Street' for silver 'far better in design and at a cost rarely exceeding that which is paid for modern plate of the same intrinsic value'. He also stressed how much more attractive was antique cutlery 'seen in the windows of a curiosity shop ' than modern plate 'cast in patterns which have no more artistic quality than the ornaments of a wedding cake'. This consumer preference for 'antique' plate is still evident today. The current production of silverware consists primarily of products in historical styles.

Even this 'antique' plate, either genuine or reproduction, represents only a small market. The once obligatory silver tea-service and canteen has gone the same way as the house-maid and butler. The modern family prefers dish-washer proof stainless steel that requires neither cleaning nor insurance. There has been a dramatic shift in patronage, away from the private individual and toward company, ecclesiastical and museum commissions. The provenance of the objects in the exhibition is proof in itself of this change. Sheer lack of patronage has created a crisis for the craft.

Graham Hughes, Art Director of the Goldsmiths' Company (1968–72) has perhaps done more than any other individual to promote 'modern' silver. He believes that 'the key to artistic style and technique is confidence and that is bred by patronage'. Robert Welch has 'no doubt that the personal relationship with customers has led to the design of many pieces of domestic silverware that might otherwise never have been produced'. Without the traditional sources of patronage where does the future of silversmithing lie?

Werner Bünck the German silversmith has eloquently summarised the situation, from his point of view as a maker

'It is regrettable that the active regard for silverware as exceptional utensils, as a festive gift, as personal eating and dining utensils, as representative pieces to be handed down – both privately and publicly – has been increasingly lost. But without doubt, this no longer lively consumer appreciation has sharpened the eye of the maker for the essence, the raison (sic) for silver articles, their relationship to sculpture and the here almost natural-seeming duty to exhibit functionally, sculpturally , and artistically.'

Some silversmiths argue that the less compulsory the utilitarian value is, the more significant the artistic handling of the form and its execution will be. For the Korean smith, Martha Sung-Won Lee the way

Opposite: *Wine Jug, 1987*
Werner Bünck (Cat. no. 65)

Below: *Tea service, 1902*
Paul Follot (Cat. no. 16)
Photo: courtesy of Bröhan-Museum

forward is through the liberation of artistic expression, to which function is subordinated. Many feel that technology can be left to cope with efficient operation and that it is the designer's job to create objects to which people can respond emotionally and sensually. An alternative route has been suggested by Klaus Dieter Eichler and Matthias Engert. They believe that the survival of the silversmith depends on becoming a designer in order to secure an income through design commissions which reach a broader class of consumers.

We have been talking very simplistically about the 'silversmith'. Even as early as the sixteenth century if not before it is clear that the word covered a variety of occupations: makers both general and those specialising in smallwork, largework, flatware, and decorative techniques such as chasing and engraving, as well as retailers and even bankers. When times were hard there is evidence to show that silversmiths worked in materials other than precious metals, they became jewellers, watchmakers and even dentists. It is worth remembering William Chaffers' description of the craft structure:

'there are necessarily in every piece of decorative plate three parties to whom the credit of production must be ascribed, viz; the artist who designs it, the plateworker who makes it, and the goldsmith who sells it and becomes the publisher.'
(Hallmarks on Gold and Silver Plate, 1883)

Today the word 'silversmith' has an even more wide-ranging definition. Some of those who learnt the craft are now experimenting with non-precious metals like steel, iron, copper and anodised aluminium. A few of the most exciting and skilful silversmiths today began their careers in other fields. Andreas Fabian took a degree in biology at Bremen, before turning to metalwork in 1991. Simone ten Hompel began her training as a locksmith and black-smith. Others are going in the opposite direction; the silversmiths John Creed and Franz Arnold are currently working in iron.

There are silversmiths like Rod Kelly who work to commission, hand crafting individual pieces for private customers. Karl Gustav Hansen has designed and made nearly 600 pieces of hollow ware for the Hans Hansen Silversmithy since 1930 – all raised by hand. Hansen asks 'Why submit to the limitations of machine production and refrain from the wealth of expression only handcrafting can offer?'. Some successfully combine designing for industry with the craft, like David Mellor, Ragnar Hansen and Brian Asquith. Robert Welch believes 'that it is possible to blend the best of these two worlds, the old and the new, the unique and the multiple, hand and machine, to the mutual advantage of each other'. Wilfried Moll has been involved in serial production for the cutlery company Robbe and Berking, where

'prototypes must indicate a final, reproducible condition. You find there are sensitive forms that are spoiled by the least deviation (and this can easily happen when someone else does the execution)'.

The combination of teaching and making has a distinguished past. Paths of influence can be identified between successive tutors, students and colleagues. Friedrich Becker has taught and influenced many silversmiths, like Werner Bünck and Johannes Kuhnen. Kuhnen's career illustrates the often complex network of mutual collaboration and inspiration. After leaving Becker in 1973 he studied under Sigrid Delius in Dusseldorf, joining Herbert Schulze in 1978 and then moved to Canberra School of Art in 1981 to work with Ragnar Hansen.

Some 'silversmiths' never formally learned the craft, but trained in other disciplines. There is a strong sculptural and architectural influence on the design of silver. Georg Jensen, Paul Follot, Jean Puiforçat and Tapio Wirkkala all began their careers as sculptors. Henning Koppel relied on the craftsmen in Jensen's workshop to realise his 'free form' silver that grew out of his fasincation for the non-figurative sculpture of Brancusi, Arp and Lamrens. The architects Mackintosh, Hoffmann, and his assistant Christa Ehrlich, Ashbee, Dawson, Wilson, van de Velde and Lauwerks all turned their intellect and imagination towards the design of silver for the table. The firm Alessi has built upon this fruitful relationship by commissioning architects like Hans Hollein and Kazumasa Yamashita to design tea and coffee services for limited production.

All these inter-relationships between function and decoration, rationality and emotion, design and industry and art and craft are under-pinned by an internationalism that has grown in strength over the twentieth century.

The last decade of the century holds both a conclusion and an exciting way forward. The silver-smiths have learnt to be as flexible as their metal.

4 Craft and Industry

Eric Turner
Assistant Curator,
Metalwork Collection
Victoria and Albert Museum

Soup Tureen, 1880
Christopher Dresser (Cat. no. 3)
Photo: courtesy of The Fine Art Society

By the end of the nineteenth century the design of mainstream silverware throughout Europe was approaching a crisis. H. Townsend in a paper delivered at the Royal Society of Arts (16 June, 1893) stated that 'Here in England we are content, not so much to attempt to revivify a corpse, as to hospitably entreat, and to be perfectly satisfied with the presence at our feasts of the mere mummy of an art…When he [the English silversmith] is a copyist, he is too often soulless; when he summons courage to be original, he is generally mindless.' A generation earlier, the Dutch silversmith J.M. van Kempen made the depressing observation in a brochure accompanying his display at the Great Exhibition of 1851; 'The workmanship of precious metals is a mere technicality, a handicraft, which every man may carry to a certain degree of perfection whereas the forms are a result of the combined art of feeling and judging, with which but few are endowed and even a whole nation, even an entire period, may be destitute of.' The international exhibitions merely helped to emphasize that while technical expertise was usually of a very high order, the talent to exploit this expertise with intelligent, innovative design was often absent.

Britain, the first European country to experience industrialisation, was also the first to suffer its disadvantages. The silver trade in an industrialized society was in an anomalous position. Neither any longer wholly craft, or yet exclusively mechanised, it occupied an uneasy position between the two extremes. Mechanized manufacture developed by the plating trades from the mid-eighteenth century onwards, inexorably influenced the traditional craft of silversmithing. Die stamps, fly punches and swage blocks enabled consistent reproduction of standard parts produced in batches. The skills initially required to set the machine tools for batch manufacture were very exacting. But once the production line was set, products could be assembled quickly by semi-skilled workers. For production in quantity of a given design, the silversmiths soon found that they were not only competing with a material that was intrinsically cheaper but the means of production was cheaper too. At first the products from the plating workshops were noticeably inferior to those of the silver trade but a comparison between a Sheffield plate candlestick of the early 1750s and one of the late 1760s shows just how quickly the platers caught up.

The British response was to appoint a Parliamentary Select Committee which convened in 1835 and reported two years later. Its remit was to propose methods of improving manufacturing standards and public knowledge of the arts and while the conclusions reached by the Committee were scarcely radical, the assumption behind its directive that a certain degree of state intervention was both necessary and desirable, was revolutionary for a Government firmly committed to free trade and a laissez faire economic policy. One immediate consequence of its investigations was the establishment of the Government School of Design at Somerset House in 1837 under the auspices of the Board of Trade. In the 1850s it transferred to South Kensington, and was amalgamated with the new Museum of Manufactures which eventually became the Victoria & Albert Museum while the School was renamed the Royal College of Art in 1896.

The South Kensington model established a pattern that was copied throughout Europe. The first was the Austrian Museum for Art and Industry (Angewande Kunst Museum) which was established in 1867 followed by the Deutsche Kunstgewerbe-museum Berlin. In Paris, the Musée des Arts Décoratifs was opened in 1877. There are many more examples throughout Germany, Holland, Eastern Europe, Scandinavia, the United States and Japan where the impetus for their foundation relied on the South Kensington initiative. Throughout Europe public collections of the industrial arts and crafts did have a direct influence on design in the latter part of the nineteenth century and throughout the twentieth.

In Britain, the Museum, its collections and the Government Schools of Design did not always fulfil their initial promise. In its early days, the School's effectiveness was compromised by a lack of clear direction which was reflected in endless disputes about the content of the curriculum. Henry Cole and his colleagues, when he was appointed Director of the South Kensington Museum and School of Design, did at least codify the school curriculum into a set of principles. They included statements such as the following; 'The true office of ornament is the decoration of utility…True ornament does not consist in the mere imitation of natural objects, but rather than in the adaption of their peculiar beauties of form or colour to decorative purposes…'

None of this by the 1850s was very new but it did at least have a reasonable degree of practicality which was Cole's essential underlying purpose. The problem was that Cole, although his organisational talents were considerable, did not have a strongly analytical mind. His principles and hence the school curriculum built on many of the recommendations of the 1835 Select Committee report which was handicapped by an overwhelming nostalgia for ancient craft traditions. It adroitly failed to address itself to the problems and complexity of industrial manufacture and Cole and Redgrave's principles took the matter no further forward. Moreover, these principles had two other basic flaws. They did not so much determine the appearance of an object but merely rationalized it and they discussed ornament as an entity outside a stylistic framework. For these reasons the relationship between the School and industrial manufacturers was not always fruitful.

However it is easy to be influenced by these criticisms and underestimate the value of the state education system at the time.

One of the most original designers of metalwork in the latter half of the nineteenth century was Christopher Dresser (1834–1904) who studied at South Kensington between 1847 and 1854. Dresser, the son of a Glasgow customs officer was from a relatively humble background and it would be fair to say that his considerable talents as a designer were wholly cultivated by the education he received as a student. Cole had a knack of attracting around him some of the most important and influential designers and theoreticians of the day and consequently Dresser was taught by the painter Richard Redgrave (1804–1888), the designer Owen Jones (1809–1874) and the German architect, Gottfried Semper (1803–1879). Jones and Semper provided Dresser with an excellent theoretical grounding while Redgrave taught him botanical drawing and instilled in him a love of the subject which in all probability encouraged Dresser to concentrate on the formal qualities of his designs more thoroughly than his contemporaries. Jones introduced Dresser to Oriental decorative art and this interest of Dresser's is more widely recognized. Dresser made a two year visit to Japan in 1876–1877 after which he produced a series of radical hollow ware designs which were manufactured by the Birmingham firms of Elkingtons and Hukin & Heath and the Sheffield firm of James Dixon and Sons. To some extent there is a discernible oriental influence, particularly in the design of the handles which can be related to the traditional bamboo handles on Japanese basket work but the explanation for their sheer originality relies on

Dresser's understanding of the structural potential of sheet metal and his thorough grounding in the functionalist principles of ornamental design which he managed to transmute into a geometrical, formal language that was truly radical.

However to say that Dresser was the precursor of the Modern movement with his hollow ware designs is to exaggerate his role. He did not inspire any immediate followers and his reputation in the broader context of his work in all other media, is that of an ornamental stylist although one of extraordinary sophistication. A greater and altogether more immediate influence on European twentieth century metalwork design was the work of Charles Robert Ashbee (1863–1942) and his Guild of Handicraft. Ashbee, trained as an architect, was strongly attracted to the ideals of William Morris (1834 –1896). They were both committed to the goals of the English Arts and Crafts Movement which sought to revive the role of the individual artist craftsman. In this respect their ambitions lay wholly outside the concerns of Cole and the South Kensington Design School which had attempted to be a co-operative venture with industry. Ashbee saw industrial manufacture as inherently corrupt, both morally and

intellectually for the workman and his public alike. He sought when he established the Guild of Handicraft in 1888 to model his studio on that of a medieval craft workshop, which was inspired by the example of Morris and the writings of the critic, John Ruskin, who viewed medieval craftsmanship as a golden age before the days of pre-industrial production. This was of course essentially a romantic concept rather than one which was based on the crude realities of medieval life or indeed the comparative sophistication of a medieval goldsmith's workshop but it was very powerful nonetheless. Ashbee's ambitions relied on the premise that the Guild should develop as a self sufficient body of independent craftsmen where each individual was responsible for the product throughout every stage of its development. So anxious was Ashbee to preserve the integrity of his craftsmen that he discouraged recruits who had any trade experience for fear that they may corrupt the others. As a result, early works by the Guild are comparatively crude and amateurish but Ashbee and his colleagues learnt quickly through an education programme wholly devised by Ashbee that interestingly drew heavily on the resources offered by the South Kensington Museum. Ashbee was not averse to drawing on historical precedent but the style of silverwork and jewellery that the Guild produced at the turn of the century was both innovative and original and relied on a simple, austere use of form and colour. Soft curves and a deliberately dull finish to the metal perfectly exploited the limitations of both his craftsmen and the material with the result that they produced a series of objects by methods which became of seminal importance to the development of silver design this century.

The Arts and Crafts Society and Ashbee in particular enjoyed considerable prestige abroad through their displays at international exhibitions such as Paris (1900) and Turin (1902) and illustrations in *The Studio* magazine which helped disseminate their ideas. The Wiener Werkstätte, founded by Joseph Hoffmann and Koloman Moser in Vienna in 1903 was inspired by Ashbee's workshop. Ashbee's Guild was however short lived for he was soon to witness others adopting his ideas and extending them further. His own success created opportunities for competitors with greater flair and more stylish designs and men such as Henry Wilson, Alexander Fisher and Arthur Gaskin were beginning to produce work which was richer and more self assured than the austere

simplicity of the Guild of Handicraft. Ashbee could only approve insofar as they were the products of small craft workshops but he was irritated by a major retailer such as Liberty launching its Cymric silver scheme which although produced on a semi industrialized basis by Haseler's of Birmingham, owed in its design a considerable debt to the pioneering work of Ashbee and his Guild of Handicraft. But whatever Ashbee's accusations, Liberty was not a plagiarizer for although its Cymric range shared certain characteristics in common, Ashbee's ideas were a point of departure. The Cymric style was a rich blend of Arts and Crafts mannerisms and continental Art Nouveau.

During the early years of this century, it can rightly be argued that British silversmithing was in the avant-garde in European silver design but this position was quickly usurped by developments in Germany. In 1907 the Deutsche Werkbund was formed, largely on the recommendations of the architect Herman Muthesius whose involvement with the British Arts and Crafts Movement made him an influential critic of German art education. The Werkbund took the ideas of the English Arts and Crafts a crucial stage further for it gave equal emphasis to artists, manufacturers and commercial interests. This in turn eventually led to the formation of the DIA (Design and Industries Association) in Britain in 1915 which broadly shared the same principles but never the same radical commitment as its German mentor and more crucially, the formation of the Bauhaus in Weimar in 1919. In its early days, under the direction of Walter Gropius, the Bauhaus in some ways resembled a medieval guild because of its emphasis on the mutual interdependence of all its activities but if its social structure resembled Ashbee's workshops, the aesthetic values it created could not have been more different. The teachings of the Bauhaus eliminated all questions of ornamental decoration and reduced design to its essentials; materials, functions and abstract relationships. The crafts were there to provide design research for industrial production. It is a little difficult to gauge just how influential the Bauhaus was at the time for it was abruptly closed in 1933 by the Nazis, before it had the opportunity to have any substantial influence within Germany itself and its staff and students dispersed. But it was to prove of enduring influence in the post war period where its principles and the models it created have been studied and emulated the world over.

The inter-war years in Britain saw the emergence of a modified form of modernism on a small scale. The most influential educative force was the Vittoria Street School, an adjunct to the Birmingham School of Art which principally sought to modify and put on a more realistic basis, the principles and practices of the Arts and Crafts Movement. The resurgence in British silversmithing came in the years following the Second World War with the renaissance of the Royal College of Art. The College was completely re-organised following a Ministry of Education report with a new emphasis placed on the needs of industry. Interestingly, this direction gave fresh impetus to the crafts taught in the College (particularly that of silversmithing) as much as it did to the needs of reviving industrial production in a post war climate. Men with now established reputations such as Gerald Benney, David Mellor and Robert Welch enjoyed distinguished careers as industrial designers as well as establishing themselves at the same time as pre-eminent silversmiths. In Scandinavia, which provided the model for this in the 1950s, the links between craft and industry were even more closely forged. Perhaps the Victorian ideals of an indivisible link between art and industry was at last beginning to be realised but the economic

Tea pot, 1993
Johannes Kuhnen (Cat. no. 81)

collapse of European industry in the last twenty years in particular has ultimately denied this development. European silversmithing for the time being has returned to being a specialized craft with a niche market with the result that there has in this generation, been an increasing emphasis on craftsmanship for its own sake. In this respect, one might argue that we have returned to the Arts and Crafts environment of a century ago but there is greater diversity nowadays for that argument to be sustained. We have, for example, a growing indigenous silversmithing tradition in Australia which has largely been led by European migrants such as Johannes Kuhnen and Ragnar Hansen. They have increasingly made sophisticated experiments with new materials which through their teaching at the Canberra School of Art has stimulated new trends. In Italy, there is the series of silver designs, produced and promoted by Cleto Munari in a modernist and post modernist manner which has largely been designed by internationally distinguished architects, a recurrent tradition in European silversmithing over centuries. In Scandinavia, the 1970s saw a resurgence of the craft tradition after twenty years of a remarkable homogeneity of craft and industrial design which

has put an increasing emphasis on manipulation of the material. The time for a retrospective survey as we near the end of this century is particularly apt because of so many exciting developments that are taking place. The fact that the craft has continued to flourish despite the many inimical pressures imposed on it this century is not only indicative of enduring appeal of silver but also the investment that has been made in the craftsman's education in the past one hundred and fifty years. For whenever a country has enjoyed particular pre-eminence in the craft, there is evidence that there has been a concomitant commitment to the education of the craftsmen and women, and their public. It is to be hoped that this exhibition forms yet another link in this process for the collection of objects assembled is to be enjoyed and serve as a stimulus to the craftspeople and public, now and for the future.

5

Inheriting Modernism
Michael Rowe Course Leader,
Goldsmithing/Silversmithing/
Metalwork/Jewellery, RCA

Box, 1978
Michael Rowe (Cat. no. 50)
Photo: David Cripps

I continue to work in metal, fascinated by its qualities as a material and by the technical processes of forming it. Over the past twenty years, my main interest has been in searching for new expression in the area of hollow ware. The absurdity of creating a piece that has an equivocal relation to function is deferred by the insistent presence of the finished thing. Questions of whether it is design or sculpture seem futile. If the concept is strong and expressed with the strictest economy, if the judgements of scale, internal coherence, proportion, finish etc. are good and as finely tuned as I can get them, then maybe the thing will sing a little and have poetic resonance. That will justify it a place in the world.

It is difficult to account accurately how visual ideas form in the imagination, we can, after all, only recall the conscious part of the process. Intuition plays a significant role in the making of choices. Kant's works still ring true. 'Concepts without intuitions are blind, intuitions without concepts are lame.' Further complexity is provided by the contribution made by language itself to the processes of creation. We can be certain that language as critique, does play an active part. Indeed it is a defining feature of modernist practice. In using the term Modernism, I am referring to a particular lineage of ideas that stretch back at least as far as the Enlightenment but which only blossomed in the early years of this century in response to the profound social and intellectual changes that occurred in Europe at that time. Central to modernism is the idea that the artist's individuality is sovereign. It followed that primary experiences and poetic perceptions could provide the immediate stuff of art and be transformed directly into paint, stone or other medium without filtration through the conventions of traditional practice. This notion opened up vast possibilities for expression. In painting, the illusionist mode of representation was suddenly inadequate as the vehicle for dealing with the fresh upsurge of messages and meanings. In architecture and design, the canon of Classical Orders came under critical review after nearly five hundred years of almost continuous authority. The abstract principles of taxis and symmetry could still be useful, but as a system of forms it was judged to be no longer relevant, a body of ossified symbols out of tune with the needs and spirit of the time. Science and technology were taking over as the essential paradigms, not only in determining the character of forms that were employed but more profoundly, in the ways these disciplines were conceived intellectually. In architecture, metaphors of science and technology replaced references to temple ritual. Across the arts, a period of intense philosophical inquiry was set in motion, questioning the fundamental nature of art, design and architecture, their processes, procedures and practise. These great introspections were documented in the form of artists' manifestos and architects' programmes, and it is no coincidence that a signifcant number of the early pioneers whose influence in creating the new modes of practise, people such as Klee, Mondrian, Kandinsky, Malevitch, van Doesburg and le Corbusier all wrote elegantly articulated treatises, employing visionary language to extol the potential of their methods for creating new visual worlds.

For me, these writings still inspire and have an admirable clarity of purpose, even though some of the vision, now realised, reveal serious flaws.

Now in this Post Modern period the paradigms have shifted again and it is information theory that provides the over-arching metaphors in cultural discourse. Global communications bring enormous quantities of visual material plundered from every corner of the world, and this eclectic intermingling is giving new hybrids. The underlying ideals of Modernism remain intact however. Each age defines its own cultural values and the unremitting roll of history continuously reinterprets those values according to its own standpoint. I know that the moves I make are firmly rooted in this continuum and that if they make sense at all, it is because of it. That relatedness is a source of their meanings.

6 Biographies

Silversmiths working today

Malcolm Appleby
b. 1946, England

Fish slice, 1990 Carcase by Peter Musgrove Engraving by Malcolm Appleby (Cat. no. 122)

Appleby trained at Ravensbourne College of Art and Design and the Central School of Arts and Crafts. After qualifying from the Sir John Cass School of Art and the Royal College of Art he set up his own workshop, first in Kent and then at Crathes near Aberdeen in 1969. He has developed fresh approaches to engraving on silver and techniques of fusing gold on to steel.

Franz Arnold
b. 1954, Switzerland
Apprenticed as a goldsmith in 1970

Arnold is presently working in Zurich in his own atelier in Schafisheim. He combines designing and making with teaching, having attended a teachers training course in 1980. He has been learning how to forge iron since 1987. Last year he received a foundation grant from Stiftung Goldener Schnitt. His silver tray draws on an organic and sculptural free-form source that can be seen in the work of Henning Koppel and the fine art trained Scandanavians.

Brian Asquith
b. 1930, England
Asquith gained a scholarship to the Royal College of Art Sculpture School in 1947. In 1955 he set up a small workshop in Sheffield to learn practical engineering. By the 1960s Asquith had started to make objects in metal which were a link with his sculptural training, experimenting with design ideas and

Tray, 1993, by Franz Arnold (Cat. no. 68)

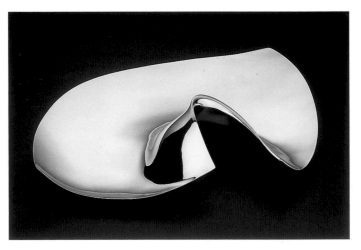

abstract form. He visited Milan and Turin in 1965 which greatly influenced his design thinking. His work remains both faithful to the craft studio movement and faces the challenge of quality product design for manufacturing companies.

Frank Bauer
b. 1942, Germany

Bauer began his apprenticeship in silversmithing in 1962. In 1966 he worked under Bertil Gardberg at the Kilkenny Design Workshops. In the later '60s Bauer studied industrial design and architecture first at the Artschool in Kassel and then at the Hochhschule für Bildende Künste in Hamburg. On arriving in Australia in 1971 Bauer worked with Wal van Heeckeren at the Argyle Arts Centre in Sydney. In 1975 the Jam Factory Workshops in Adelaide engaged Bauer. Between 1979 and 1984 Bauer moved to London, lecturing at Middlesex, Surrey and Sir John Cass Schools of Art. On returning to Adelaide Bauer became lecturer in Metalsmithing and Jewellery at the South Australian

Three goblets, 1990
Brian Asquith (Cat. no. 69)

Coffee pot, 1987
Frank Bauer (Cat. no. 63)

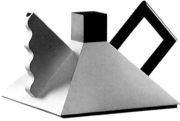

School of Advanced Design. He is now concentrating on serial production work. Bauer's work derives in part from the Bauhaus influence of a return to basic geometric volumes but with a very personal freedom of combination.

Simon Beer
b. 1956, England

Simon Beer was apprenticed to David Mellor, and was awarded a Diploma in Silversmithing, Jewellery and Engraving from the Sir John Cass School of Art. After setting up in partnership with the jeweller Jonathan Swan he built his own workshop in Lewes, East Sussex. Since being awarded the commission for the Southwark Cathedral church plate in 1981 Beer has concentrated on ecclesiatical projects. He has just been awarded a Churchill Fellowship for study in Japan. Beer draws inspiration from architectural detailing and describes his work as 'very pure and simple, like gravestones'.

Gerald Benney

b. 1930, England

Gerald Benney trained under Dunstan Pruden in the workshop complex at Ditchling, Surrey, founded by Eric Gill, and at Brighton College of Art. He started his own workshop on graduating from the Royal College of Art in 1955, where he became Professor of Silver-smithing and Jewellery from 1974 to 1983. In 1957 he was appointed consultant designer to Viners of Sheffield. From 1963 he has worked from Beenham House in Berkshire. Benney works mainly in the field of handmade silver and gold articles using various texturing techniques, and high temperature fine enamels.

Cutlery, 1991 Gerald Benney (Cat. no. 119)

Rudolf Bott

b. 1956, Germany

Between 1972 and 1975 Bott trained as a goldsmith in Hanau and spent his journeyman years there and in Raesfeld from 1975 to 1978. From 1980 to 1983 he worked in collaboration with M. Pollinger in Munich. Since 1983 he has been studying at the Akademie der Bildenden Künste in Munich. He set up his own workshop in Munich in 1989. *The work is distinguished by its artistic and intellectual quality. The hollow mounted napkin rings exhibit an independent solution for everyday workmanship, and the sensitive handling of the surface deserve special notice. Set symbolically in space these are not just napkin rings, but rather small objects in themselves. (Silbergestaltung, 1992, p.208)*

Napkin ring, 1991
Rudolf Bott (Cat. no. 70)

Werner Bünck

b. 1943, Germany
Bünck completed his apprenticeship in 1963. He studied product design for four years under Professor Friedrich Becker at the Werkkunstschule in Dusseldorf from 1967. Between 1970 and 1972 he worked as a designer for the glass and porcelain industries. Since 1973 he has worked as a freelance silversmith in combination with teaching appointments first at the Fachhochschule in Dusseldorf and from 1980 as Professor for Metal Design at the Facchochschule in Hildesheim. In 1988 and 1991/2 he was guest lecturer at the Royal College of Art. He has swiftly developed his own style, that is bound to a technically informed asthetic.

'Emphatically contemporary, unadorned, unassuming, but not bound to the spirit of the age. From a range of historical silver utensil types he purpose-fully chooses the elemetary forms – bowls, pots, receptacles, utensils, and systematically explores formative aesthetic and functional conditions.'
Gerhard Dietrich on Werner Bünck in *The Eloquent Vessel. Three Silversmiths – Three Countries*, 1992.

Andrew Bray

b. 1938, England
Andrew Bray was awarded a National Diploma in Design (Special Level) from Canterbury College of Art in 1961. He graduated from the School of Silversmithing and Jewellery at the Royal College of Art in 1964. Bray is a Fellow of the Society of Designer Craftsman, Freeman of the Worshipful Company of Goldsmiths and of the City of London. He has taught at Canterbury College of Art, Kent College, Middlesex Polytechnic and is now Director of Silversmithing and Metalwork at Camberwell College of Arts. His work can be seen in Cambridge College Collections at Clare, Corpus Christi and Churchill, and in several Livery Company collections in London.

Bray has worked on commissions for Ministries, Federations, Associations and

Fruit dish, 1993
Andrew Bray (Cat. no. 71)

Societies as well as industrial commissions including a range of cutlery *Sipelia* for a Sheffield firm, knives for Kitchen Devils and has developed prototype lighters for Ronson and Dunhill. He continues to research and develop his own work. His dish exploits the unique qualities of silver. The dark oxidised panels contrast dramatically with the alternate highly polished strips.

Dish, 1992
Clive Burr (Cat. no. 72)

Tea pot, 1987
Werner Bünck (Cat. no. 66)

Clive Burr
b. 1953, England
Clive Burr began his training at Loughborough College of Art graduating with a first class degree from High Wycombe College of Art in 1973. On graduating from the Royal College of Art in 1979 he set up his own workshop, and now operates from Berry Street in London. Burr is best known for his elaborate and highly decorative clocks. He is also concerned with the design and production of silverware and jewellery either as production runs, exclusive ranges, or special 'one-off' commissions. His design work includes projects completed for Garrard, Mappin and Webb, Next Directory and Retail and Thomas Goode.

Kevin Coates
b. 1950, England
After studying music in Australia and England Kevin Coates completed his foundation studies at West Sussex College of Design. He was awarded a Diploma in jewellery design from the Central School of Art in 1973. Three

years later he graduated from the Royal College of Art. He has maintained his involvement with baroque music throughout his career, playing, broadcasting and researching. His Ph.D. completed in 1979 is a study of the use of mathematics in musical instrument design. Coates work demonstrates a mastery of carving, modelling and casting allied to a rich world of allegory, symbolism, art and science.

Xavier Corbero
b. Spain
Xavier Corbero is one of Spain's foremost avant-garde sculptors and lives just outside Barcelona. His father owned one of the biggest chasing factories in the country. It was during Corbero's early training as a silversmith at the Centre of Arts and Crafts that he produced the jug on display. His subsequent career has been a reaction against the discipline.

Jug, 1957 Xavier Corbero (Cat. no. 41)

John Creed
b. 1938, England
Creed was awarded a National Diploma in Design from Liverpool College of Art, and undertook industrial training at Walker and Hall silversmiths in Sheffield. Between 1966 to 1971 he produced decorative, small scale silverwork and jewellery from his own workshop in Yorkshire, as well as

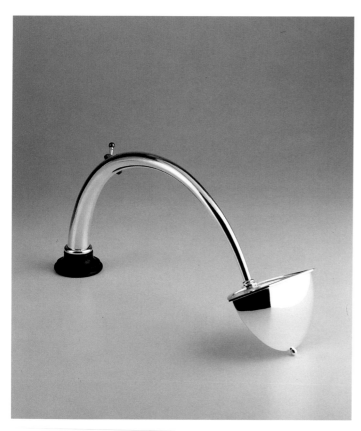

teaching in Glasgow.

A study trip to the USA in 1988 resulted in a radical change of direction to working with large scale objects in forged steel. Since that time he has undertaken a number of public commissions and is represented in many collections, as well as continuing to design and make both iron and silver objects for domestic interiors.

Rebecca de Quin
b.1958, England

After completing her Foundation Course in Art and Design at Barnet College in 1985 Rebecca de Quin was awarded a first class honours degree from Middlesex Polytechnic in 1988 in Three Dimensional Design. Since graduating from the Royal College of Art in 1990, she has won many awards for domestic silverware including those sponsored by the Goldsmiths' Company and *House and Garden*. She is a visiting lecturer at the Royal College of Art and teaches part-time at Middlesex University. The

46

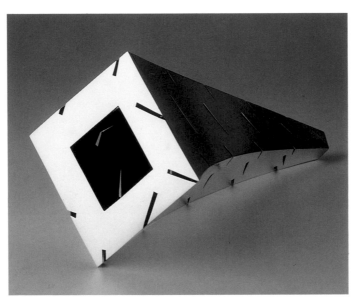

Pomander, 1992
Rebecca de Quin (Cat. no. 73)

'dialogue' between inner and outer
parts of a form motivates much of her
work, which is based on the use of
pierced pre-fabricated sheet silver,
folded and soldered into shapes.

Stuart Devlin

b. 1931, Australia
Devlin worked for two years as
designer craftsman in silver at T. Gaunt
& Company in Melbourne. He taught in
art schools in Victoria and was
awarded the Diploma of Art from the
Royal Melbourne Technical College. In

Tea pot, 1972
Stuart Devlin (Cat. no. 45)

1958 he was awarded a grant to
study in Britain graduating from the
Royal College of Art three years later.
He designed the Australian decimal
currency. He now exports all over the
world, basing himself mostly in London.
Until 1984 he had as partner the Duke
of Westminster. Devlin was one of the
first silversmiths to exploit the limited
edition in silverware. In 1977 he sold
his workshop to Hector Millar.

Leslie Durbin

b. 1913, England

Trained in the workshops of Omar Ramsden and at the LCC Central School under Augustus Stewars before the Second World War. Following the War he set up his own workshop in partnership with Leonard Moss, whilst also teaching at the Royal College of Art and the Central School. Durbin produced designs in silver which combined simplicity with a degree of sumptuousness and decorative detail which did not conform to the taste of the time for plain simple forms.

Fish slice, 1990
Leslie Durbin (Cat. no. 109)

Andreas Fabian

b. 1957, Germany

Andreas Fabian studied biology at the University of Bremen before training in metalwork at Fachhochschule in Hildesheim. In 1991 he graduated from the Department of Silversmithing and Jewellery at the Royal College of Art. Since 1992 he has worked as a freelance designer and silversmith. His work reveals a pronounced personal technique allied to clear form, and a confidence in proportion. Objects made by Fabian have been exhibited in Hanau, London, Hildesheim, Bremen, Zurich and Antwerp.

Cutlery, 1991
Andreas Fabian (Cat. no. 115)

Howard Fenn

b. 1953, England

Howard Fenn was awarded a Diploma with distinction in Design and Craftsmanship of Silver from the Sir John Cass School of Art. After leaving college he worked for the silversmith John Norgate, mainly producing work for the Middle East. In 1979 he set up his own workshop in Rotherhithe near Tower Bridge, combining work and teaching. Fenn's work is easily recognisable with its bold clear lines, proportion and sculptural qualities. Apart from working all in silver, he regularly combines it with other materials, particularly slate.

Felix Flury

b. 1959, Switzerland

Studied silversmithing at the Sir John Cass School in 1986, graduating from the Royal College of Art in 1989. He operates from his workshop in Recherswil, Switzerland.

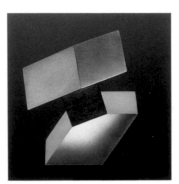

Salt & pepper, 1993
Felix Flury (Cat. no. 76)

Max Frölich
b. 1908, Switzerland
Between 1924 and 1925 Frölich
trained at the Ecole des Arts Industries in
Geneva and then at the Kunstgewerbe-
schule in Zurich where 'the basic
attitude, the critical questioning of the
practicability and mangeability of an
item intended to be used and handled',
has stayed with him ('Silversmith,
Designer or Artist?', in *Silbergestaltung,*
Klinkhardt & Biermann, 1992, p.144).
He worked as a journeyman between

1928 and 1934 in Lucerne, Brussels
and Zurich. Since 1934 he has worked
freelance from his own workshop.
He has been assistant teacher, Head
of the Metal Class and then Assistant
Director of the Gewerbeschule in
Zurich, retiring in 1974.

Pot, 1986
Wolfgang Gessl (Cat. no. 62)

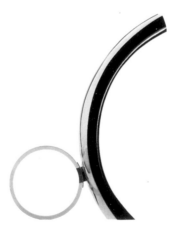

Wolfgang Gessl
b. 1949, Austria
Studied goldsmithing under Professor
Hans Angerbauer in Austria and with
Sigurd Persson in Stockholm at the
National College of Art, Craft and
Design. In 1978 he graduated from the
National College returning to teach
metalwork and jewellery. He now works
from his workshop in Stockholm. His
work is in private collections in Sweden,
Germany, Norway, Switzerland,
Austria, Australia and Japan.

Karl Gustav Hansen
b. 1914, Denmark
Karl Gustav Hansen, son of the founder
of the Hans Hansen Silversmithy in
Kolding, Denmark, and its director and
chief designer since 1940, has made
important contributions to the Danish
silver style from the early 1930s to the
present. In 1930 Hansen was
apprenticed to Einar Olsen, winning
in 1934 the silver medal, the highest
distinction in the Danish apprenticeship
system for his test piece, a tea pot.
Shortly afterwards he enrolled at the

School of Sculpture at the Art Academy as a pupil of Utzon Frank, but continued to work in silver. He has been living in Switzerland since 1970 and has a workshop there.

Why submit to the limitations of machine production and refrain from the wealth of expression which only handcrafting can offer? Raised silver has an incomparable quality - it is alive. And there is also the economic aspect. I am not keen on large editions, so it costs you less, or not more at any rate, to raise a form by hand than to prepare all the necessary tools.
('Sixty Years of Holloware' in *Silbergestaltung*, 1992, p.150)

Ragnar Hansen
b.1945, Norway
After completing his silver apprentice-ship at Norway Silver Design, Hansen worked for the Kilkenny Design Workshop in Ireland with responsibility for training apprentices. Between 1970 and 1972 he worked for Norway Silver Designs on mass production designs and special commissions. In 1972

Ragnar Hansen arrived in Australia to join the Sturt Metal Workshop at Mittagong, New South Wales. The following year he set up gold and silversmithing courses at the School of Art at the Tasmanian College of Advanced Education. In 1981 he was invited by the Canberra School of Art to establish Australia's first and only post-graduate school of silversmithing and jewellery. In 1988 he convened the First International Silversmithing Symposium at Canberra School of Art. Ragnar Hansen transferred the Scandanavian sculptural tradition to an Australian context.

Hans Hollein
b.1934, Austria
Studied at the Academy of Fine Arts in Vienna until 1956. He graduated from Chicago and the University of California at Berkley in 1960. As one of the most influential architects of his age he was invited by Alessi to design a prototype for a tea and coffee service.

Tea service Aircraft Carrier, *Alessi prototype 1984* Hans Hollein (Cat. no. 54)

Rod Kelly

b. 1956, England

Rod Kelly graduated with a first class
Honours Degree in Three Dimensional
Design from Birmingham Polytechnic.
In 1983 he left the Royal College of Art
and now works from his home in Norfolk.

Kelly makes up all his designs using
traditional techniques. Most of his
pieces are hand raised from flat circles
of silver. The design for decoration is
drawn on the surface of the silver with
a pencil ready for embossing. Flat
chasing is Rod Kelly's speciality and
his low relief images, hammered into
the silver are his trademark. When
designing he thinks of the function and
the decoration of the silver in tandem
and likes to include elements pertinent
to the prospective customer or the event
to be celebrated.

Pair of Vases, 1992
Rod Kelly (Cat. no. 59)

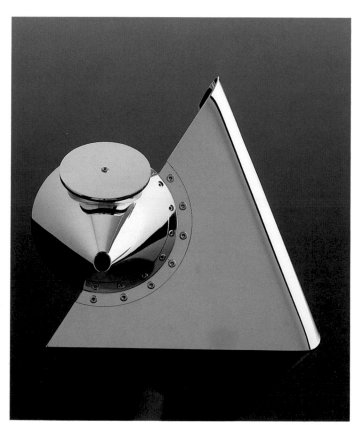

Christopher Knight

b. 1964, England

Chris Knight graduated from Sheffield
City Polytechnic in 1987 with a first
class degree in Three-Dimensional
Design specialising in Silversmithing
and Jewellery. At the Royal College of
Art he became interested in using the
computer as an aid to design. He now
works from the South Bank Crafts Centre
designing and producing to commission
and batch production for retail outlets.
His current work centres around the
manipulation of the cone form.

Tea pot prototype, 1992
Chris Knight (Cat. no. 79)

Johannes Kuhnen

b. 1952, Germany

Apprenticed to Friedrich Becker
between 1969 and 1973 Kuhnen
subsequently studied under Sigrid Delius
at the Fachhochschule, Dusseldorf
between 1974 to 1978. From 1978
he set up a workshop jointly with
Herbert Schulze and Helen Aitken-
Kuhnen in Dusseldorf. Three years after

moving to Australia in 1981 Kuhnen joined Ragnar Hansen at the Canberra School of Art. His work reflects the cool precision of modern German practice, using a combination of simple geometric forms executed with superb precision. Today he is best known as a gold and silversmith working in anodised aluminium and silver.

Tea pot, 1993
Johannes Kuhnen (Cat. no. 81)

Helge Larsen
b. 1929, Denmark
In 1946 Larsen began his apprenticeship in jewellery with Viggo Wollny in Copenhagen and was awarded his National Diploma in 1950. In 1955 he set up in conjunction with Harold Jensen a workshop, Sølvform. In 1961 Helge Larsen left Denmark to settle in Australia joining the Department of Industrial Arts at the University of New South Wales in Sydney. He established a jewellery and silversmithing partnership with his Australian born wife Darani Lewers. The range of hollow ware they made exemplified the simple organic forms and largely undecorated surfaces characteristic of contemporary Scandanavian silversmithing. In 1978 Larsen set up the Jewellery and Silversmithing Department of the recently established Sydney College of Arts, becoming in 1988 its Deputy Director. He is now Head of the School of Visual Arts.

Darani Lewers
b. 1936, Australia
After attending the Jewellery Apprenticeship Course at East Sydney Technical College Darani Lewers became a trainee at Sølvform in 1959. She is married to Helge Larsen.

Michael Lloyd
b. 1950, England

Fish slice, 1990, M Lloyd (Cat. no. 117)

Lloyd trained in Birmingham and at the Royal College of Art, completing his MA in 1976. In 1975 he was awarded a RCA travelling scholarship. He currently lives and works in Kirkcudbrightshire in Scotland, and was awarded a Scottish Development

Agency Craft Fellowship in 1991. He makes hand raised and constructed forms. His methods also include chasing both on three-dimensional forms and in negative for printmaking. His work can be seen in the collections of the Crafts Council, the Contemporary Arts Society and the Worshipful Company of Goldsmiths. He has received commissions for Goldsmiths' Hall, Lichfield Cathedral and the Royal Society and from the Silver Trust for 10 Downing Street. Michael Lloyd is a Freeman of the Worshipful Company of Goldsmiths.

Alistair McCallum

b. 1953 England

Alistair McCallum has made a special study of mokumé gane, a traditional Japanese metalworking technique which has been in use for some 300 years. Briefly the technique involves the bonding of copper, copper alloys and silver through a series of processes, resulting in a decorative wood grain effect.

Fish slice, 1990,
A McCallum (Cat. no. 116)

Pair of goblets, 1993 (unfinished)
Robert Marsden (Cat. no. 82)

Robert Marsden

b. 1947, England

Marsden studied silversmithing at High Wycombe College of Technology and Art, gaining his Diploma in 1969. From there he went to the Royal College of Art, where he completed his MA in 1972. For the next fifteen years he lived in London and Sheffield where he helped to set up workshops, finally setting up his present workshop in Hackney in 1987. Marsden does not strictly design his work but rather works through an idea which he translates into form. He is technically proficient, the inspiration for his work owing much to structural engineering and industrial metalworking. He has experimented with various shapes and his latest work has seen the assemblage of disparate geometric and free-formed shapes with differences in surface and finish, which are also functional.

54

Ulla Mayer
b. 1948, Germany
Between 1970 and 1975 studied at
the Akademie der Bildenden Künste in
Nuremberg under Professor E. Hößle,
setting up her own workshop in 1976.

David Mellor
b. 1930, England
Studied silversmithing at the Sheffield
School of Art (1946-48), gaining a first
class Diploma at the Royal College
of Art before finishing his academic
studies at the British School in Rome
(1953 –54). In 1954 he set up his
own workshop and design consultancy.
As a consultant designer to Walker and
Hall he was awarded a Design Centre
Award in 1957 for his *Pride* cutlery
service, which is now considered an
English classic. In 1975 he converted
historic Broom Hall to purpose designed
workshops for the specialist production
of David Mellor cutlery.

*Having trained as a silversmith, I
tend to think of myself primarily as a
maker. My work as an industrial designer,
developing prototypes for quantity*

Pride *cutlery, 1957*
David Mellor (Cat. no. 105)

*production, has been balanced by
my work as a craftsman, making special
one-off pieces of silver. My approach
to design is still, to some extent, that
of a craftsman, in my involvement in
directing all the detail and in making a
design concept work from end to end.*
David Mellor in *Contemporary
Designers*, 1983.

Ljubisa Misić
b. 1948, Yugoslavia
Ljubisa Misić's early career as a ceramic
designer is studded with various awards.
After learning the craft between 1972
and 1975 Misić went on to study at the
Fachhochschule für Keramik Gestaltung
in Höhr-Grenzhausen. The 'triangle'
cutlery designed for the firm C. Hugo
Pott Besteck-fabrik in Solingen, Germany
won a major international award.

Anna Moll

b. 1964, Germany

After leaving the Sorbonne in Paris in 1984 Anna Moll began her training as a silversmith at the State Crafts College in Neugablonz. On graduating in 1987 she joined the Summer Academy in Salzburg studying under Nele Bode and continued her training with Peter Müller in Munich. In 1988 she became a guest student at the Montgomery Community College in Maryland, USA in the class of Professor Komelia Okim. She opened her own workshop in 1990. Her work can be seen at the Gallery Treykorn in Berlin.

Bowl, 1993, by Anna Moll (Cat. no. 83)
Cutlery, Ljubisa Misić (Cat. no. 114)

Wilfried Moll

b.1940, Germany

Moll was apprenticed in Hamburg and spent his journeyman's years in Copenhagen. He studied at the Akademie der Bildenden Künste in Nuremberg under Professor Andreas Moritz, receiving a Diploma in 1965. Since then he has worked jointly with Gerda Mo from his own workshop in Hamburg. He has been working on serial production projects with the silver manufacturers Robbe and Berking.

In designing for serial production, some rethinking is necessary. While the charm of the purely accidental is valued in a one-of-a-kind piece, protoypes must indicate a final reproduceable condition. You find there are sensitive forms that are spoiled by the least deviation (and this can easily happen when someone else does the execution). Other forms are more resistant and retain their validity; here the strengths of the silversmith bear results. He can make changes rapidly and unproblematically, produce a series of variations, and compare them with each other. In his work method, the direct

Can, 1986 Paul Müller (Cat. no. 86)

connection between head and hand, the silversmith has tremendous advantages over operations with elaborate, co-operative specialization.(Wilfried Moll 'Silversmithing: Passion and Profit', in Silbergestaltung, 1992, p.163)

Paul Müller

b.1956, Germany

Between 1972 and 1975 Müller was apprenticed near Augsburg winning first prize in a national competition. He attended the Fachoberschule für Gestaltung in Augsburg between 1975-6. After graduating as a goldsmith in 1981 he studied at the Academy of Fine Arts in Nuremberg under Professor Hößle. In 1984 he became one of the five founder members of 'Gruppe Buntmetall', a group of students and graduates dedicated to creating awareness of silver hollow and flatware through exhibitions. From 1988 he has worked from his own studio in Nuremberg.

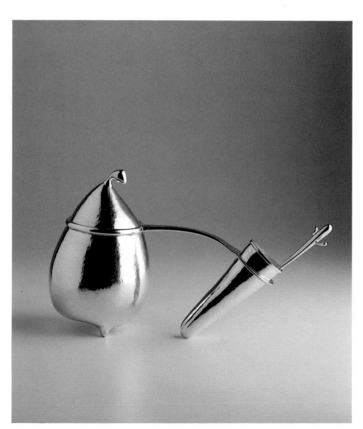

Karen Murray

b. 1966, England

Karen Murray was awarded a BA in Design, specialising in Silversmithing and Jewellery from Glasgow School of Art in 1990. While a student she studied enamelling in Limoges. She completed her MA at the Royal College of Art in 1992. She now works at the same workshop as Laurence Pugh. Commissions include individually designed bowls, a coffee pot and spoons, as well as batch produced tableware.

Marmalade pot and spoon, 1990
Karen Murray (Cat. no. 87)

Kevin O'Dwyer

b. 1953, Ireland

Kevin O'Dwyer was awarded a Higher National Diploma in Biotechnology from Waterford in 1975. He began a jewellery and enamelling apprenticeship with Harriet Dreissigger in 1979, joining William Frederick in 1982 to train as a silversmith. From 1982 he has maintained a private

58

studio in Dublin specializing in silver and jewellery commissions. Since 1989 he has been a Design Methods Lecturer at the National College of Art and Design in Dublin. His work is in many permanent collections including the High Museum Atlanta Georgia, Ulster Museum Belfast, University of Georgia, Swiss Embassies in Beijing and Paris and in the private collections of President Mitterrand and King Juan Carlos.

Louis Osman
b. 1914, England
Graduated from the Bartlett School of Architecture in 1935 and underwent training as a medallist before turning his attention to silver works within an Arts and Crafts tradition . He is one of the few major silversmiths of his generation who did not go to the Royal College of Art or have any experience with industrial design. Between 1970 and 1980 Osman operated from Canons Ashby in Northampton-shire. Osman now lives and works at Byford Court near Hereford.

Left: Cutlery, 1972
Louis Osman (Cat. no. 108)

Above: Tea pot from Mad Hatter's
Tea Party *sevice, 1992*
Kevin O'Dwyer (Cat. no. 88)

Yukie Osumi
b. 1945, Japan
Graduated from the Faculty of Fine Arts, Tokyo National University of Fine Arts and Music in 1969. Her special subject was the history of metal crafts. After graduating Osumi practised metal-work techniques and artistry under Ikkoku Kashima and Shiro Sekiya (Living National Treasures) and Moriyuki Katsura. In 1988 she was a awarded a Fellowship under the Japanese Government Overseas Training Programme for Artists and studied at the British Museum and the Victoria and Albert Museum until 1989.

Laurence Pugh
b. 1967, England
While on the Three-Dimensional Design course at Middlesex Pugh began to explore the potential of architectural metalwork, working in iron and glass. Since graduating from the Department of Silversmithing and Jewellery at the Royal College of Art, he has been working on commissions from a workshop shared with Karen Murray in Bow, East London. His work has been sold to clients in America, Spain, Italy, Japan and Hong Kong. He thinks of his highly figurative silver as 'classic tableware with a twist'.

Justin Richardson
b. 1967, England
Steven Ottewill
b. 1968, England
Justin Richardson and Steven Ottewill met at the Kent Institute of Art and Design where they were both awarded the BTEC Higher National Diploma in Silver-smithing. They have worked for Naylor Brothers, and Kent based silversmtihs Padgham and Putland, Ian Calvert, J.C. Birtles and N.V. Bassant. They have set up in partnership operating from Evegate Farm in Smeeth, Kent.

Pair of water pitchers, 1990
Richardson & Ottewill (Cat. no. 91)

60

Michael Rowe
b. 1948, England
Graduated from High Wycombe
College of Art with a first class honours
Diploma in Art and Design, and from
the Royal College of Art in 1972.
Between 1976 and 1982 Rowe was
a visiting lecturer at Camberwell School
of Art. While there he researched, in
collaboration with Richard Hughes,
the colouring, bronzing and patination
of metal. In 1984 he was appointed
Course Leader of Silversmithing and
Jewellery at the Royal College of Art.
His work is in many public collections
including Birmingham City Museum,
Crafts Council London, Leeds City Art
Gallery, Victoria and Albert Museum,
Badisches Landesmuseum in Karlsruhe,
Germany, and the Art Gallery of
Western Australia,

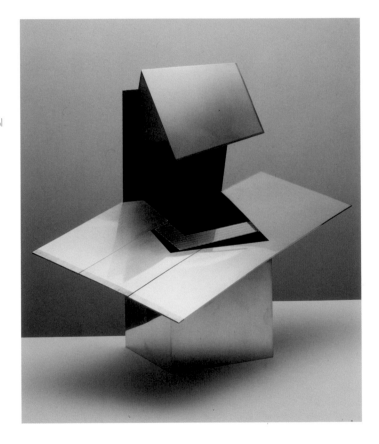

Vessel, 1993
Michael Rowe (Cat. no. 51)

Lino Sabattini

b. 1925, Italy

After attending elementary school
Sabattini worked in a Como shop
selling brass knick-knacks. Inspired by
the Gio Ponti's magazine *Domus* he
moved to Milan at the age of thirty,
where he set up a metal working shop.
Ponti admired his work, publishing it
in *Domus* and helped him exhibit at
the Milan Triennales from 1954 to
1959. From 1956 to 1963 Sabattini
was appointed director of a new line
'Formes nouvelles' for Christofle.
In 1964 Sabattini left Milan and
returned to Como where he opened his
own silversmithy, with about twenty-five
apprentices. He sells mostly to private
clients, or to progressive international
retailers like Rosenthal. Lino Sabattini
regards the fabrication of useful
objects as a creative act, he stresses
design over problems of production
and emphasizes aesthetics over the
limitations of industrial production.

Fenice *tea service,* 1989
Lino Sabattini (Cat. no. 67)

61

Allan Scharff

b. 1945, Denmark
Between 1963 and 1967 Scharff was apprenticed in the workshop of the Georg Jensen Sølvsmedie in Copenhagen. From 1973 to 1975 he studied at the Danish College of Jewellery, Silversmithing and Professional Trade Design in Copenhagen, where he was later

Watercock jug, 1992
Allan Scharff (Cat. no. 93)

at intervals deputy teacher. From 1975 to 1978 Scharff worked as an independent silversmith, also acting as art advisor to the Hans Hansen Sølvsmedie in Kolding. The following year was spent in the workshop of the Museum of Art in Herning. He worked freelance in his own workshop on the island of Enceleave near Horsens between 1979 and 1983. Since 1985 he has been based once again in Copenhagen. His designs are sculptural and witty, he is a master at creating shapes inspired by natural forms, particulary birds.

Herbert Schulze

b. 1953, Germany
Studied at the Fachhochschule in Dusseldorf under Professor Sigrid Delius and Professor Friedrich Becker. Schulze believes that *'the design of utensils moves within the tension between industrial, product, and object design, and the fine and applied arts'*, ('Hollow and flatware design at the Fachhochschule Dusseldorf', *Silbergestaltung*, 1992, p.111)

Tea pot with warmer, 1993
Herbert Schulze (Cat. no. 94)

Jane Short

b. England
Whilst training as a jeweller at the Central School of Art and Design, Jane Short was introduced to enamelling. After studying silversmithing at the Royal College of Art she set up a workshop as an enameller, making both jewellery and silverware, always enamelled.

Short divides her time between commissioned work, exhibition work, teaching and enamelling for other goldsmiths. Short exhibits mainly through the Crafts Council at the Victoria and Albert museum and the Oxford Gallery, Shipley Art Gallery and the National Museums of Scotland.

Gisbert Stach

b. 1963, Germany
Between 1984 and 1987 Stach was apprenticed at the Fachschule für Glas und Schmuck in Kaufbeuren-Neugablonz. After completing his apprenticeship he studied under Professor Peter Skubic at the Fachhochschule für Kunst und Design in Cologne. Since 1991 he has been studying with Professor Otto Künzli at the Akademie der Bildenden Künste in Munich.

Tea pot, 1987
Gisbert Stach (Cat. no. 64)

Rose Stach

b. 1964, Germany
Rose Stach has studied at the Fachschule für Glas und Schmuck in
Kaufbeuren-Neugablonz and the
Fachhochschule für Kunst und Design
in Cologne. Since 1990 she has been
working freelance from her own workshop in Munich.

Left: Candelabra, 1993
Rose Stach (Cat. no. 95)

Below: Centre piece, 1983
Alex Styles (Cat. no. 56)

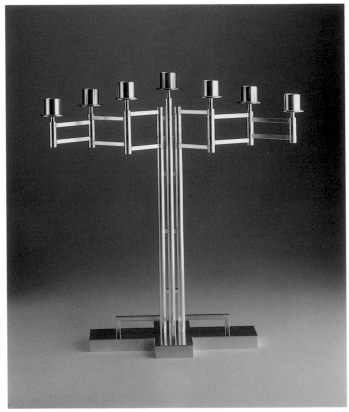

Alex Styles
b. 1922, England
Alex Styles studied at Gravesend
Technical College and Gravesend
School of Art. He learned the technical
aspects of design from Leslie Bottomly
at the Central School of Arts and Crafts.
In 1947 he joined the Goldsmiths and
Silversmiths Company designing a
great and varied range of silverware,
from regalia to domestic tableware.

Lucian Taylor
b. 1967, England
Lucian Taylor graduated with a first class
honours degree in Three-Dimensional
Design from Brighton Polytechnic in
1989 and proceeded to the Royal
College of Art, graduating in Goldsmithing in 1992. He now works from
Oxford. His bone end cutlery combines
fly-press forging with lost-wax casting.

Cutlery, 1992, Lucian Taylor
(Cat. no. 120)

Simone ten Hompel
b. 1960, Germany
In 1975 Simone ten Hompel was
apprenticed as a locksmith and
blacksmith in Germany. After
graduating from the Department of
Jewellery at the Fachhochschule in
Dusseldorf she worked as a jeweller
and goldsmith for various businesses.
After deciding not to continue as a
jeweller she won a place at the Royal
College of Art to pursue her interest in
silversmithing. Since graduating in
1989 she combines teaching at the
Sir John Cass and Camberwell College
of Art with making from her workshop in
Clerkenwell Green. She acknowedges
that her *work is the result of influences
from my own surroundings and from
other cultures... [I] consider the relationship between form and function vital t
o a piece and always endeavour to find
a balance between these aspects that
satisfies my own personal aesthetic
values. My choice of material is
based on its tactile and visual nature
which often results in my use of combined materials within one object.*

Left: Sugar and cream set, 1992
Simone ten Hompel (Cat. no. 98)

Right: Salt and pepper, 1993
Richard Vallis (Cat. no. 99)

Richard Vallis
b. 1964, England
Vallis studied at West Surrey College
of Art and Design, graduating in 1987
with a degree in Three Dimensional
Design in Metal. Three years later he
was awarded an MA in Metalwork
and Jewellery from the Royal College
of Art. Since 1991 he has worked on
various commissions in conjunction with
the David Gill Gallery in London. He
combines making with restoring antique
metalwork and clock restoration with
work as a technician at Camberwell
College of Art. He is currently visiting
lecturer at Loughborough College
of Art. Vallis is particularly interested in
combining different materials and
techniques such as folding, casting,
electro-forming and spinning.

Jan van Nouhouys
b. 1949, Holland

After training at the Middlebare Technische School 'Vakschool Schoonhoven' van Nouhouys worked as a silversmith in the Hague from 1971 to 1974. He spent the next year with a leading silversmith in London. Since 1976 he has been working freelance in the Hague from his own atelier. In 1978 he began teaching at the 'Vakschool Schoonhoven'.

Christina Weck
b. 1942, Germany

Christina Weck graduated from the Akademie der Bildenden Künste in Nuremburg in 1969. The following year she set up a workshop in Munich. From 1974 she has been a Master of Goldsmithing. Her work is represented in many museums.

Robert Welch
b. 1929, England

Tea pot, 1974
Robert Welch (Cat. no. 49)

Studied firstly under Cyril Shiner and R.G. Baxendale at the Birmingham College of Art before continuing with his post graduate work at the Royal College of Art which he completed the same year as Gerald Benney. He won a scholarship to visit Sweden in 1954 where he first came into contact wth Sigurd Persson. In 1955 he was appointed as a consultant designer to Old Hall Tableware of Bloxwich in the Midlands. Welch alongside his consultancy work set up his own silversmithing workshop in Chipping Campden in Gloucestershire in the same premises occupied by C.R. Ashbee and the Guild of Handicraft in the early years of this century. He has achieved a career equally balanced between the requirements of industrial design and the craft of silversmithing.

I believe that it is possible to blend the best of these two worlds, the old and the new, the unique and the multiple, hand and machine, to the mutual advantage of each other. Robert Welch in *Hand and Machine*, 1986, p.17.

Kazumasa Yamashita
b. Japan

Yamashita is a prominent Japanese architect who was invited by the Italian company Alessi to contribute to their Tea and Coffee Piazza, a collection of tea and coffee services designed by well-known architects. Other contributors to the 'Piazza' include Alessandro Mendini, Michael Graves and Mario Bellini.

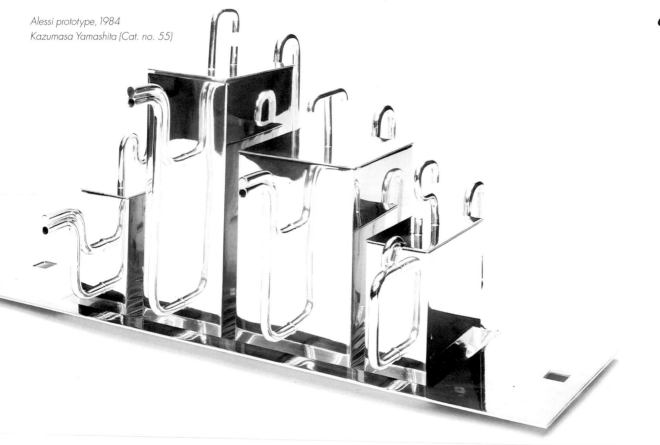

Alessi prototype, 1984
Kazumasa Yamashita (Cat. no. 55)

7

Exhibition list
Dimensions in centimetres

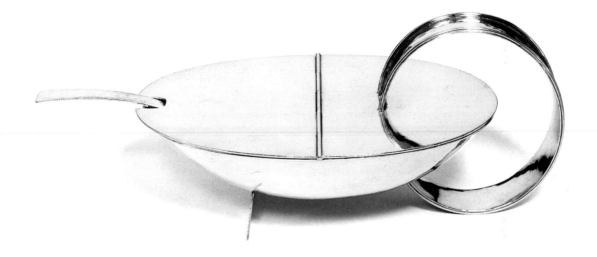

Opposite: Flower basket, 1906–1907,
Josef Hoffmann (Cat. no. 8)
Photo: courtesy of the British Museum

Above: Parmesan dispenser, 1930,
Robert Fischer (Cat. no. 31)
Photo: courtesy of Bröhan-Museum

'TL'
17th century, English

1 TEAPOT 1670/71,
Silver H34.5
Victoria and Albert Museum
Illustrated: P.Glanville, *Silver in England,*
London: Unwin Hyman 1987, p.67 fig.25.
The earliest known English silver teapot,
constructed from a cone of metal.

George Wickes
1698–1761 English

2 TEA SERVICE 1993 designed 1745,
Silver H max 19.75
Made by Garrard
Garrard
Illustrated: Elaine Barr, *George Wickes
1698–1761 Royal Goldsmith* London:
Studio Vista/Christie's, 1980,
p.114 fig.68.
The popularity of reproduction silver is
illustrated by this tea service of 1745,
produced by the founder of the firm, and in
production today.

Christopher Dresser
1834–1904, English

3 SOUP TUREEN, 1880
Electro-plate with ebony knob and handle
H23 W31.3 Diam 23
Made by Hukin and Heath, Birmingham
Andrew McIntosh Patrick
Similar illustrated: Stuart Durrant, *Christopher
Dresser,* Academy Editions 1993

4 EGG STEAMER, 1884–1885
Silver and ebony H20
Made by H. Stratford, Sheffield
(1834–1904)
Victoria and Albert Museum
Illustrated: *Silver of a New Era,* Rotterdam,
Museum Boymans-van Beuningen 1992,
Cat. no.3, p.19

5 TEA POT, 1880
Electro-plate with ebony handle H 23
Made by James Dixon and Sons
Andrew McIntosh Patrick
Illustrated: Widar Halen,
Christopher Dresser. Oxford, Phaidon
Christie's half-title

6 SKETCHBOOK, 1880s
Paper H3 W15 D25
*Ipswich Borough Council Museums and
Galleries*
Illustrated: Widar Halen 'The Dresser Pattern
Books from Charles Edward Fewster's
Collection', *The Journal of the Decorative
Arts Society 1850 to the Present*
No.12 pp.1–9.

7 DESIGN BOOK,
Elkington and Company, 1880s
Paper
Victoria and Albert Museum
Illustrated: Adrian Tilbrook 'Christopher
Dresser: designs for Elkington and
Company' *The Journal of the Decorative Arts
Society 1850 to the Present*
No.9 pp.23–28.

Josef Hoffmann
1870–1956, Austrian

8 FLOWER BASKET, 1906-7
Silver and glass H24 W4.2
Made by Wiener Werkstätte
Designed c.1905
The British Museum
Illustrated: Judy Rudoe *Decorative Arts
1850–1950 A Catalogue of the British
Museum Collection* British Museum Press
1991 p.56 Cat. no.123.
This architect and designer was the founder
of the Vienna Secession, and one of the
pioneers of functional design. His work
developed partly under the influence of
C. R. Mackintosh.

Jan W. Eisenloeffel
1876–1957, Dutch

9 TEA SERVICE, 1903
Silver H max 21.5 Diam (tray) 28
Made by Fa.Stoffels & Company
Private Collection
Illustrated: Annelies Krekel-Aalberse *Art
Nouveau and Art Déco Silver* London:
Thames and Hudson 1989
Cat. no.167 p.182.

C.R.Ashbee
1863–1942, English

10 SUGAR BASIN, 1906
Silver H7.8 W11.5
Made by Guild of Handicraft
Cheltenham Art Gallery and Museum
Illustrated: Annette Carruthers *Ashbee to
Wilson The Hull Grundy Gift to
Cheltenham Art Gallery and Museum*
Part 2, 1986, Cat. no.21.

11 MUFFIN DISH WITH LINER AND COVER,
1900–1901
Matt silver set with three chrysophrases;
Made by Guild of Handicraft
Victoria and Albert Museum
Illustrated: Eric Turner Modernism and
English Silver *V&A Album* Victoria and Albert
Museum 1989, fig.4, p.243.
Architect, designer and leader of the Arts
and Crafts Movement. He founded the
Guild of Handicraft in 1888.

Nelson Dawson
1859–1942, English

Edith Dawson
1862–1928, English

12 BOWL AND COVER, 1902
Silver and enamel H7.6 W 9.4
Cheltenham Art Gallery and Museum
Illustrated: Annette Carruthers *Ashbee to
Wilson The Hull Grundy Gift to Cheltenham
Museum and Art Gallery*
Part 2, 1986, Cat. no.32.

Henry Wilson
1864–1934, English

13 CHAFING DISH, 1908–1909
Silver, part gilt H30
Victoria and Albert Museum
Illustrated: *Silver of a New Era* Rotterdam
Museum Boymans-van Beuningen 1992,
Cat. no.18, p.34

Archibold Knox
1864–1933, English

14 VASE (for Liberty & Co), 1902
Silver and tuquoise cabochons H23 W12
John Jesse

Orfèvrerie Christofle
Founded 1830, French

15 BREADBASKET, 1900
Silver; H1.35 D W
Private Collection
Illustrated: *Silver of a New Era* Rotterdam
Museum Boymans-van Beuningen 1992,
Cat. no.46, p.55

Paul Follot
1877–1941, French

16 TEA SERVICE, 1902
Silver and ivory H27.5
Made by I. W, Quist
Bröhan-Museum, Berlin
Illustrated: *Metallkunst vom Jugendstil zur
Moderne* (1889–1939)
Bröhan-Museum Berlin 1990,
Cat. no.180, p.185

Henry van de Velde
1863–1957, Belgian

17 PLATE, 1906
Silver H21.5 W21 L21.5
Made by Theodor Müller, Weimar
Private Collection
Illustrated: Annelies Krekel-Aalberse *Art
Noveau and Art Déco Silver* London:
Thames and Hudson 1989,
Cat. no.133 p.161

J.L.Mathieu Lauweriks
1864–1932, Dutch

18 DISH, 1913
Silver H11
Made by Frans Zwollo Sr and the Hagener
Silberschmeide
Private Collection
Illustrated: Annelies Krekel-Aalberse *Art
Nouveau and Art Déco Silver* London:
Thames and Hudson 1989, Cat. no.162

Johan Rohde
1856–1935, Danish

19 LIDDED BOWL, 1914
Silver H13
Made by Georg Jensen
Georg Jensen Museum
Illustrated: Georg Jensen *The Danish
Silversmith* 1986 Cat. no.43

Robert Johnson
English

20 TEAPOT *Cube*, 1922–1923
designed 1916
Silver and wood H13 W13 L13
Made by Napper and Davenport
Victoria and Albert Museum
Illustrated: *Silver of a New Era* Rotterdam
Museum Boymans-van Beuningen 1992,
Cat. no.23 p.36
Patent originally lodged on November 13
1916 by Robert Johnson of Leicester, several
years before the first Bauhaus designs for
metalwork.

Christian Dell
1893–1974, German
21 WINE EWER, 1922
Silver and ebony H20.1
Bauhaus Archiv Berlin
Illustrated: *Die Metallwerkstatt am Bauhaus*,
Bauhaus Archiv 1992 Cat. no.140, p. 193
In 1922 appointed Handwerklicher Meister
of the metal workshop of the Bauhaus.

Marianne Brandt
1893–1983, German
22 TEA-INFUSER WITH STRAINER, 1924
Silver and ebony H7.3 W16.1 diam 10.6
Made by the Bauhaus Metal Workshop
The British Museum
Illustrated: Judy Rudoe *Decorative Arts
1850–1950 A Catalogue of the British
Museum Collection* British Museum Press,
1991, Cat. no. 26 p.276

Wilhelm Wagenfeld
1900–1990, German
23 SAUCE DISPENSER WITH UNDERPLATE
1924
Silver and ebony H16 W15.5
Bauhaus Archiv Berlin
Illustrated: *Die Metallwerkstatt am Bauhaus*
Bauhaus Archiv, 1992,
Cat. no. 318, p.294

Carl Christian Fjerdingstad
1891–1968, Norwegian
24 BOWL, 1925
Silver H8 L18.5
Made by Orfèvrerie Christofle, Paris
Musée Bouilhet-Christofle
Illustrated: *Silver of a New Era* Rotterdam
Museum Boymans-van Beuningen 1992,
Cat. no. 53 p.64

Delheid Frères
from 1925, Belgian
25 CENTRE PIECE, c.1925
Silver, mirror, glass and ebonised wood
H9 L56 W28 with tray
John Jesse

Christa Ehrlich
b.1903, Austrian
26 TEA SERVICE, 1928
Silver H16.5
Made by Zilverfabrik Voorschoten
Private Collection
Illustrated: Annelies Krekel-Aalberse *Art
Nouveau and Art Déco Silver* London:
Thames and Hudson 1989,
Cat. no. 180, p.187
Christa Ehrlich was Assistant in Hoffmann's
architectural practice. From 1927 she
designed modern silver for the
Zilverfabrik Voorschoten. Cylindrical forms
were made in a limited number of
diameters, with and without covers, spouts
and ears in several heights.

Johan Rohde
1856–1935, Danish
27 PITCHER, 1925–1932 designed 1920
Silver H23.5 W12.7
Made by Georg Jensen
Private Collection
Illustrated: Annelies Krekel-Aalberse *Art
Noveau and Art Déco Silver* London:
Thames and Hudson 1989,
Cat. no.211 p.227
This pitcher was made five years after it was
designed as it was at first thought too
modern.

Georg Jensen
1866–1935, Danish
28 BOWL, 1926
Silver H15 W20 L36
Georg Jensen Museum
Illustrated: *Silver of a New Era* Rotterdam
Museum Boymans-van Beuningen 1992,
Cat. no.202 p. 230

Jean Després
1889–1980, French
29 BOWL, 1930
Silver W11
Private Collection
Illustrated: Annelies Krekel-Aalberse *Art
Nouveau and Art Déco Silver* London:
Thames and Hudson 1989, Cat. no.70

Harald Nielsen
1892–1977, Danish
30 PITCHER, 1933–1934
Silver H15.5 D15.3
The British Museum
Illustrated: Judy Rudoe *Decorative Arts
1850–1950 A Catalogue of the British
Museum Collection* British Museum Press
1991, Cat. no.233 p.268
Nielsen joined Georg Jensen in 1909 and
was art director of the Sølvsmedie after
Jensen's death in 1935.

Robert Fischer
1906–1941, German
31 PARMESAN DISPENSER, 1930
Silver
Made by Ernst Treusch
Bröhan-Museum Berlin

Svend Weihrauch
b.1899, Danish
32 WINE EWER, 1933
Silver H22
Made by Frantz Hingelberg
Bröhan-Museum Berlin
Illustrated: *Metallkunst vom Jurgendstil zur
Moderne (1889–1939)* Berlin 1990,
Cat. no.230 p.227
Weihrauch worked for Frantz Hingelberg
from 1928.

Sigvard Bernadotte
b.1907, Swedish
33 JUG, 1938
Silver H15.2
Made by Georg Jensen
Bröhan-Museum Berlin
Illustrated: *Metallkunst vom Jugenstil zur
Moderne (1889–1939)* Bröhan-Museum
Berlin 1990 Cat. no.280 p.274

Theodor Wende
1883–1968, German
34 MOCHA SERVICE, 1930
Silver with carved ivory handles
H23 W37.5
Badisches Landesmuseum
Illustrated: Annelies Krekel-Aalberse *Art
Nouveau and Art Déco Silver* London:
Thames and Hudson 1989,
Cat. no. 152, p.152

Jean-Emile Puiforçat
1897–1945, French
35 ORANGE JUICE DISPENSER, 1930
Silver and wood H26
Bröhan-Museum Berlin
36 TUREEN, 1937
Silver
Bröhan-Museum Berlin
Illustrated: *Metallkunst vom Jugendstil zur
Moderne (1889–1939)* Bröhan-Museum
Berlin 1990, Cat. no.452, p.399
Puiforçat, like the Bauhaus designers,
based his new forms on the sphere, the cone
and the cylinder, but the results are very
different. The forms and structure of
Puiforçat's objects reveal his leaning towards
sculpture, something he shared with his
colleagues, the silversmiths Georg Jensen
and Johan Rohde.

Maurice Muller
b.1907, French
37 TETE-À-TETE, 1930
Silver and ebony H11
Made by Bloch-Eschevèque
Bröhan-Museum Berlin
Illustrated: *Metallkunst vom Jugendstil zur
Moderne (1889–1939)* Bröhan-Museum
Berlin Cat. no.452, p.399

Harold Stabler
1872–1945, English
38 TEA SERVICE, 1935
Silver, wood and ivory; H8.3 W7.6 L19.8
Made by Adie Brothers, Birmingham
Victoria and Albert Museum
Illustrated: Eric Turner 'Modernism and
English Silver' *V&A Album* 1989, Victoria
and Albert Museum 1989 fig. 39, p.42
One of Stabler's designs for mass
production. This service is entirely
geometric in character and typical of
the Art Déco style.

Henning Koppel
1918–1981, Danish
39 PITCHER, 1952
Silver H28.7
Made by Georg Jensen
Georg Jensen Museum
Hand raised and sculpted reflecting the
designer's training at the Royal Danish
Acdemy of Fine Arts in Copenhagen.
40 BOWL, 1956 designed c.1950
Silver H16.2 W39.5
The Worshipul Company of Goldsmiths.
Illustrated: Claude Blair (ed) *The History of
Silver* Macdonald & Company 1987,
p.209
This piece shows Koppel's mastery
of assymmetrical sculptural free-form
Modernism.

74

Xavier Corbero
Spanish
41 JUG, 1957
Silver H22 W18.3
The Worshipful Company of Goldsmiths

Lino Sabattini
b.1927, Italian
42 TEA/COFFEE SERVICE *Como*, 1957
Silver H max 17.75
Made by Christofle, Paris
Musée Bouilhet-Christofle
Illustrated: Claude Blair (ed.) *The History of
Silver* Macdonald & Company 1987,
p.210
Como won a prize at the exhibition Formes
et Idées d'Italie held in Paris in 1957.
It remains one of the most eccentric and
idiosyncratic examples of 1950s
Italian style.

Gerald Benney
b.1930, English
43 TEA/COFFEE SET, 1964–1966
Silver H max 24
Fitzwilliam College Cambridge
Illustrated: P. Glanville *Silver in England*,
London: Unwin Hyman 1987,
p.262, fig.106
Commissioned by the first fellows and some
friends of Fitzwilliam College.

44 TEA POT *Saddleback*, 1961
Silver H14
Victoria and Albert Museum
This teapot was made for a limited
competition in 1961 for a silver service to be
made for the use of British Embassies
abroad. It encorporates his distinctive
textured surface decoration that became a
characteristic of that period.

Stuart Devlin
b.1931, Australian
45 TEA POT *England*, 1963
Silver and wood H17 W26.5
Made by Wakely and Wheeler
The Worshipful Company of Goldsmiths.

David Mellor
b.1930, English
46 TEA POT AND MILK JUG *Embassy*, 1963
Silver with black fibre handle H18 max
Victoria and Albert Museum
Winner of the British Embassies' silver
competition. An example of the 1960s
British governments conversion to the
'modern' style.

Helge Larsen
b.1929, Danish

Darani Lewers
b.1936, Australian
47 BOWL, 1966
Silver H7
*The Trustees of the Museum of Applied Arts
and Sciences, Sydney.*

Tapio Wirkkala
1915–1985, Finnish
48 BOWL, 1971
Silver H6.5
Auran Kultaseppa Oy

Robert Welch
b.1929, English
49 TEA POT, 1974
Silver H13
Crafts Council Collection
Illustrated: Robert Welch *Hand and
Machine* Chipping Campden 1986, p.30

Michael Rowe
b.1948, English
50 BOX, 1978
Silver with copper edge H24.5 W13 D18
Crafts Council Collection
51 BOX, 1978
Silver, red gold H25 W33 D20
Private Collection

Christina Weck
b.1942, German
52 BOX, 1980
Silver H12 W9.5
Badisches Landesmuseum

Ulla Mayer
b.1948, German
53 PLACE SETTING, 1980
Silver H24 W24 L22.5
Badisches Landesmuseum

Hans Hollein
b.1934, Austrian
54 TEA SERVICE *Aircraft carrier*, 1983
Silver HDW
Made by Alessi
Victoria and Albert Museum

Kazumasa Yamashita
b1937, Japanese
55 TEA SERVICE prototype, 1983
Silver
Made by Alessi
Victoria and Albert Museum

Alex Styles
b.1922, English
56 MULTI-PURPOSE CENTRE PIECE, 1983
Silver H23 W49.5
Made by Garrard
Garrard
Alex Styles worked in the design department
of the Goldsmiths' and Silversmiths'
Company from 1947, and later for
Garrard for over forty years. His work,
mainly 'one-offs', was first executed by the
firm of Wakely and Wheeler, and later by
Naylor Brothers.

Johannes Kuhnen
b.1952, German
57 BOX, 1984
Silver H2.5 L11.5
*The Trustees of the Museum of Applied Arts
and Sciences, Sydney.*

Max Frölich
b.1908, Swiss
58 TEA POT, 1984
Silver H17

Rod Kelly
b.1956, English
59 PAIR OF VASES, 1985
Silver H30.5
Garrard

Ragnar Hansen
b.1945, Norwegian
60 COFFEE POT, 1985
Silver H23.5
*The Trustees of the Museum of Applied Art
and Sciences, Sydney.*

Jan van Nouhouys
b.1946, Dutch
61 TEA POT, 1985
Silver H12 W12

Wolfgang Gessl
b.1949, Swedish
62 POT, 1986
Silver with acrylic handle H34.5 W10
Vestlandske Kunstindustrimuseum

Frank Bauer
b.1942, German
63 TEA POT, 1987
Silver H12.5 W18.5
*The Trustees of the Museum of Applied Art
and Sciences, Sydney.*

Gisbert Stach
b.1963, German
64 TEA POT, 1987
Silver, ebony and maplewood
H13.5 W21.5

Werner Bünck
b.1943, German
65 WINE JUG, 1987
Silver and ebony H26.5 Diam 19
66 TEA POT, 1987
Silver H18.5 Diam 10

Lino Sabattini
b.1927, Italian
67 TEA SERVICE *Fenice*, 1989
Silver
Rosenthal

Franz Arnold
b.1954, Swiss
68 TRAY 1993
Silver H10 W45 L65

Brian Asquith
b.1930, English
69 GOBLETS, 1993
Silver & acrylic H17
Glaxo Holdings plc

Rudolf Bott
b.1956, German
70 NAPKIN RINGS 1991
Silver H4 D5

Andrew Bray
b.1938, English
71 BOWL FOR FRUIT 1993
Oxidised and polished silver
H30 W30 L30

Clive Burr
b.1953, English
72 DISH 1992
Silver Dia 33

Rebecca de Quin
b.1958, English
73 FOUR SIDED POMANDER 1992
Silver strip with gold plated interior
H8 W8 L23
74 CONE POMANDER 1990
Silver strip H11 W11 L25
© RCA

Howard Fenn
b. 1953, English
75   HINGED BOX 1990
Silver and slate   H15 W22 D12

Felix Flury
b. 1956, Swiss
76   SALT AND PEPPER 1993
Silver and wood   H7 W7

Karl-Gustav Hansen
b. 1914, Danish
77   MILK JUG 1991
Silver   H21.8
78   CANDLESTICK FOR SIX CANDLES 1993
Silver   H16.4 W19

Chris Knight
b 1964, English
79   TEA POT 1993
Silver and gilt (prototype: chrome)
H22 W25 D20
80   TWO PITCHERS 1992
Silver   H25 W17 L17
Straight cone: © RCA

Johannes Kuhnen
b. 1952, German
81   TEA POT 1993
Silver and anodised aluminium
H26 W16 D17

Robert Marsden
b. 1947, English
82   PAIR OF GOBLETS ON BASE 1993
Silver and patinated copper
H21 W35 L30

Anna Moll
b. 1964, German
83   BOWL 1993 designed 1990
Silver and semi-precious stones   H7 W2.5

Wilfried Moll
b. 1940, German
84   TEA POT 1992 designed 1991
Silver and wood   H12.7
85   SUGAR BOWL, CREAMER, TRAY, AND
WARMER 1992
Designed 1991
Silver   H max 8.5 L max 23

Paul Müller
b. 1956, German
86   CAN 1986
Silver   H30 W18 D7
Werner Gmell

Karen Murray
b. 1966, English
87   MARMALADE POT AND SPOON 1992
Silver and silver gilt   H19 W20

Kevin O'Dwyer
b. 1953, Irish
88   TEA POT AND JUG
Mad Hatter's Tea Party 1992
Silver   H29 W15 D10, H19 W8 D4.5

Yukie Osumi
b. 1945, Japanese
89   VASE 1990
Silver   H31.5
Victoria and Albert Museum

Laurence Pugh
b. 1967, English
90   CENTREPIECE 1993
Silver   H60 W30 D20

Justin Richardson
b. 1967, English

Steven Ottewill
b. 1968, English
91   TWO JUGS 1990s
Silver
Made by Justin Richardson

Allan Scharff
b. 1945, Danish
92   Flycatcher 1990
Silver   H8 W11 D6.5
93   Watercock 1992
Silver and aluminium
H20.5 W16.5 D11.5

Herbert Schulze
b. 1953, German
94   TEA POT WITH WARMER 1993
Silver, glass and ebony   H28.5 W13 D21

Rose Stach
b. 1964, German
95   CANDELABRA 1993 designed 1990
Silvered brass   H37 W41.5 L12

Simone ten Hompel
b. 1960, German
96   VINEGAR AND OIL SET 1991
Silver   H max 23.5
Victoria and Albert Museum
Commissioned and loaned to the V&A by
the Makower Trust.
97   FLASK 1992
Silver   H18 W4 D3
98   SUGAR AND CREAM SET 1992
Silver on mild steel base   H17 W4 D5.5
Max base L30
Private Collection

Richard Vallis
b. 1964
99   SALT AND PEPPER 1993 designed 1991
Silver and gilt interior   H max 19

Exhibition List
Cutlery

Cutlery, Magnolia 1919
Georg Jensen (Cat. no. 102)
Photo: courtesy of Bröhan-Museum

Charles Rennie Mackintosh
1868–1928, Scottish
100 MEAT FORK, PUDDING SPOON, SOUP
SPOON, 1902
Silver L max 26.8
The British Museum
Illustrated: Judy Rudoe *Decorative Arts
1850–1895- A Catalogue of the British
Museum Collection* British Museum Press
1991, Cat. no. 147, p.215

Josef Hoffmann
1870–1956, Austrian
101 SNAIL PICK, CRAB FORK, CHEESE KNIFE,
FRUIT KNIFE, 1906
Silver and silvered alpacca L max 17.9
Made by Wiener Werkstätte and
Bachmann & Company
The British Museum
Illustrated: Judy Rudoe *Decorative Arts
1850–1959 A Catalogue of the British
Museum Collection* British Museum Press
1991, Cat. no.124, p.250

Georg Jensen
1866–1935, Danish
102 3 SPOONS, FORK, PICKLE FORK
Magnolia, 1919
Silver L max 23.8
Bröhan-Museum Berlin
Illustrated: *Metallkunst vom Jugendstil zur
Moderne (1889–1939)* Bröhan-Museum
Berlin 1990 Cat. no. 254 p.254

Omar Ramsden
1873–1939, English
103 SLICE, 1921
Silver L28
Prof B S Rabinovitch

David Mellor
b.1930, English
104 KNIFE, FORK, DESSERT, SOUP AND TEA
SPOONS *Embassy,* 1957 designed 1954
Silver L max
105 KNIFE, FORK, DESSERT SPOON *Pride*
1957 designed 1954
Silverplate

Robert Welch
b.1929, English
106 TEA, SOUP AND DESSERT SPOONS,
TABLE AND DESSERT FORKS, TABLE AND
DESSERT KNIVES *Alveston* (relaunched as
RW NO 1), 1962
Silver L22
Illustrated: Robert Welch *Hand and
Machine* Chipping Campden 1986,
p.124–5
107 FOUR SPOONS, TWO FORKS, TWO
KNIVES *Premier* 1983
Silver L22
Made by Harrison Fisher Ltd Sheffield for
Coutier Ltd

Louis Osman
b.1914, English
108 KNIFE, FORK AND SPOON, 1972
Britannia silver and 18ct gold L fork 23..5
The Worshipful Company of Goldsmiths

Leslie Durbin
b.1913, English
109 FISH SLICE AND FORK, 1990, 1992
Silver L30.5, L26
Prof B S Rabinovitch

Simon Beer
b.1956, English
110 KNIFE, FORK AND SPOON
Silver L max 22
K B Page

Tapio Wirkkala
b.1915–1985, Finnish
111 KNIFE, FORK AND TWO SPOONS
Composition
Silver and stainless steel
Rosenthal

Arne Jacobsen
1902–1971, Danish
112 KNIFE, FORK, DESSERT AND TEA SPOON
1990s
Silver and stainless steel
Rosenthal

Lino Sabbatini
b.1927, Italian
113 KNIFE, FORK AND TWO SPOONS
Sculptura
Silver and stainless steel
Rosenthal

Ljubisa Misić
b.1948, Yugoslavian
114 KNIFE, FORK, DESSERT AND TEA SPOON
Silver plate
Rosenthal

Andreas Fabian
b.1957, German
115 KNIFE, FORK, SPOON 1991
Silver and stainless steel
© RCA

Alistair McCallum
b.1953, English
116 FISH SLICE 1992
Silver L39.5
Prof B S Rabinovitch

Michael Lloyd
b.1950, English
117 CAKE SLICE 1992
Silver L36.5
Prof B S Rabinovitch

Johannes Kuhnen
b.1952, German
118 CUTLERY 1992
Silver and stainless steel L (max) 22

Gerald Benney
b.1930, English
119 TWO KNIVES, TWO FORKS,
FIVE SPOONS 1992 designed 1961
Silver L max 25

Lucian Taylor
b.1967, English
120 KNIFE, FORK AND SPOON 1992
Silver and stainless steel L max 23
© RCA
121 KNIFE, FORK AND SPOON *Drop* 1992
Silver and stainless steel

Malcolm Appleby
b.1946, English

Peter Musgrove
b.1946, English
122 FISH SLICE 1990
Silver L28.5
Engraved by Malcolm Appleby
Prof B S Rabinovitch

John Creed
b.1938, English
123 PUNCH LADLE
Silver and nylon L30

Kevin Coates
b.1950, English
124 TART SLICE 1992
Silver L24
Prof B S Rabinovitch

Jane Short
b.1950, English
125 FISH SLICE
Silver and enamel
Prof B S Rabinovitch

78 8 **Select bibliography**

Anderson, Nola
Directions–Silversmithing 1989
Contemporary Hollow ware in Australia:
Finding the Rules
Australia 1989

Bröhan, Karl
Metallkunst vom Jugendstil zur Moderne
(1889–1939)
Berlin: Bröhan-Museum 1990

Bury, Shirley
'The Silver Designs of
Dr. Christopher Dresser'
Apollo, December 1962, p. 766

Crawford, Alan
CR Ashbee Architect, Designer and
Romantic Socialist
New Haven and London:
Yale University Press, 1985

Dresser, Christopher
Principles of
Decorative Design 1873

Goldsmiths' Company
Explosion–Talent today 1327–1977
London: Goldsmiths' Company 1977

Goldsmiths' Company
British Goldsmiths of Today
London: Goldsmiths' Company, 1992

Glanville, Philippa
Silver in England
London: Unwin Hyman 1987.

Halén, Widar
Christopher Dresser
Oxford: Phaidon, Christie's 1990

Hughes, Graham
Modern Silver Throughout
the World 1880–1967
London 1967

Krekel-Aalberse, Annelies
Art Nouveau and Art Déco Silver
London: Thames and Hudson, 1987

Naylor, Gillian
The Bauhaus Reassessed. Sources and
Design Theory
London: The Herbert Press 1985

Rudoe, Judy
Decorative Arts 1850–1950
A Catalogue of the
British Museum Collection
London: British Museum Press 1991

Theophilus
De Diversis Artibus
c.1122, edited and translated
C R Dodwell, London 1961

Turner, Eric
'Modernism and English Silver'
V & A Album
Victoria and Albert Museum 1989

Weber, Christianne (ed.)
Silbergestaltung Zeitgenossische formen
und tendenzen
Munich: Klinkhardt and Biermann 1992

Weber, Klaus
Die Metallwerkstatt am Bauhaus
Berlin: Bauhaus-Archiv 1992

Welch, Robert
Hand and Machine
Chipping Campden 1986

Acknowledgements

The Crafts Council would like to thank all those who have made this international exhibition possible especially:

Annelies Krekel-Aalberse
The Archive of Art and Design, Victoria and Albert museum
Auran Kultaseppä Oy
The Trustees of the Museum of Applied Arts and Sciences, Sydney (The Power House)
Badisches Landemuseum, Karlsruhe
Alan Bainbridge
Bauhaus – Archiv, Berlin
Brian Beaumont-Nesbitt
Besteckmuseum Bodo Glaub
Birmingham Mueseums and Art Gallery
Musée Bouhillet – Christofle
The Trustees of the British Museum
Bröhan – Museum, Berlin
Crafts Council of Ireland
Dr. Hansjörg Budliger, President of the Crafts Council (Switzerland)
Cheltenham Art Gallery and Museums
Richard Copley-Smith
Danish Museum of Decorative Art
Fitzwilliam College, Cambridge
The Fine Art Society
Garrard and Co. Ltd,. The Crown Jewellers
Georg Jensen Museum
David Gill
Glaxo Holdings plc
Werner Gmell
Ipswich Borough Council Museums and Art Galleries
John Jesse
Kunstgewerbemuseum, Berlin
Stephen Matthews
Andrew McIntosh Patrick

P&O Makower Trust
KB Page
Rosenthal Studio-House
Royal College of Art
Vestlanske Konsindustrimuseum, Bergen, Norway
The Trustees of the Victoria and Albert Museum
The Worshipful Company of Goldsmiths
Nelson Woo

We are also grateful to those who have given technical advice and assistance especially:
Nicolette Aubury
Brian Griggs
Axel Lapp
Professor Thomas Puttfarken
Matthew Wells of Techniker

Photography:
David Cripps
assisted by Paul Westbrook
Cat. nos 27, 56, 59, 64, 65, 66, 67, 69, 70, 71, 72, 73, 76 , 82, 83, 86, 87, 88, 91, 95, 98, 99, 114, 115, 119, 120, 123.